Dr. Thomas Michael

THE SECRET

DR. THOMAS

MICHAEL

The

_____

Secret

The Secret

Dr. Thomas Michael

Falcon Publishing

Arlington, Texas

A Subsidiary of Thomas Michael Ministries

The Secret
ISBN 9703932-0-2
Copyright (c)2002
Dr. Thomas Michael

Published by:
Falcon Publishing Co.
P.O. Box 200367
Arlington, TX 76006
United States of America

Cover Design by Dr. Thomas Michael

Book Production by
Jason Countryman - Pocket-Pak

FALCON PUBLISHING

FOREWORD

"The Secret" contains elements of suspense much like a good murder mystery!

Dr. Thomas Michael runs the gamut of human emotions, carries the reader from lows to highs like a "top gun pilot", goes from nadir to zenith. It plumbs Holy Writ in a new and different way.

Most clergy would play it safe. Dr. Thomas Michael departs the safe zone to lead the reader into an understanding of things long hidden by those who would not take us outside the "box" of orthodoxy.

Please, be assured; you will never be the same again. The Secret? Read and discover for yourself.

Colonel E. H. Jim Ammerman

DEDICATION

With great honour and utmost gratitude, I dedicate this book to my precious mother, Mary M. DeLaGarza, who taught me the Word of God as a child; and now that I am old, I have not departed from it. Thank you for your unselfish love, your support, and your faith in me. You are a one of a kind woman of God. A champion among women, a mother to all who fall into your embrace. You have taught me how to live above the level of mediocrity and to never compromise my convictions. I love you.

❦

SPONSORS:
~GOLD PARTNERS~

JOE & LORENA RODARTE
ERNEST & LIDIA YBARBO
NADIA & TRINA GAMEZ
RODNEY & ROBIN MALLARD

~SILVER PARTNERS~

LOUIS & PAM PEREIRA
ANITA-LOUISE.
LOUIE & LIZZETTE GONZALES
O.K. McCULLOUGH (DAD)
MELANIE HART
MICHAEL DAVID SCHILPP II
PASTORS SPIKE & SYLVIA MALDONADO &
NEW LIFE INTERNATIONAL

Thank you for your faith in this book.

CONTENTS

ACKNOWLEDGMENTS

I am truly a blessed man. I have often said, I know not one man more blessed than myself. God has graciously surrounded me with numerous people who believe in every dream I have. I am encompassed by a great bunch, who encourage me, affirm me, provide honest feedback (sometimes, brutally honest), and always treat me like a king.

A special thanks to the Agreement Center; you were my agreeable factor when writing The Agreement, and you remain faithful. Thank you from the bottom of my heart.

My staff: associate pastors, Thomas and Dana DeAndrea; Youth Minister, Ripley Scott Lanier; Blenda Gamez, Melanie Hart, Zina Sanchez, Trina Gamez (a special thanks to you, for being the "Comma Queen" and for the grammatical support you provide, not to mention all the other incidentals you so graciously handle without complaining), Jeff T. Kuhn, and the first "Honour-Bearer", Michael David Schilpp II; you are one of God's greatest gifts to me. Thank you for giving yourself completely to the purpose of God; remember, "We're in this together." My utmost appreciation to all of you for your questions that probe deeper into the wisdom within me that often convincingly cause me to rewrite, even when I don't want to.

To the most beautiful woman in all the world, my wife, Judy, thank you for allowing me the time and space to pursue the promptings of the Holy Spirit, which lead me to write the mysteries of His Word. Our best days are just ahead. Thank you for wearing the many hats you wear at home and abroad. I never question the sleepless nights I spend at the office producing and writing, whether our children will miss out on anything because you provide them with more than enough.

To my precious little angels, Katherine Ariel and Carrington Alexander, I am always so proud of you both. You are the best at everything you do; you make me look like the world's greatest father. You two are the finest kids a father could ask for. I will always passionately love you, "Katty" and "Zander".

Respectfully, to the Holy Spirit, the Knower of all truth, I honour Your glory in my life. Thank You for speaking to me daily. You knew from the beginning that I would come along and yield to Your power; may You always find in me a heart willing to pen what is on Your heart.

And finally, to you - my readers. A celebratory thank you for taking the time to read each word carefully penned to bring you into the light of what God has spoken to my heart. May you experience the same joy and enthusiasm I felt when writing this book as you read along.

INTRODUCTION

A revolution has begun.

It is a revolution of people ready to fulfill their purpose and destiny. A revolution of uncommon champions. Champions, not because of any great natural feats or demonic defeats, but because of their willingness to meet the Father's request for worship. It is not an overstatement to describe this revolution as a movement that is sweeping across a globe filled with much hatred, jealousy, contention, and division in need of a touch from Heaven.

The greatest plague known to man is not in the form of manifested catastrophes, such as world wars and terrorism, nor the destruction of many lives through disease, famine, or natural disasters. We are faced with a far more devastating evil than that of human extinction; we are faced with the challenge of spiritual annihilation. Each year tens of thousands of believers enter eternity without ever realizing their true destinies. Although tens of thousands each year come to the saving knowledge of Jesus Christ, few ever come into the knowledge of the true purpose of the Church. The culprit is not some *flesh* sin, but rather, a hidden principle, a hidden factor that ravages many with the fire of its torrid destructive power.

The secret is about to be revealed.

The secret that has kept so many from living the abundant life for which Jesus willingly gave His life.

Open your heart and receive the light that shines brightly illuminating the obscurity of ignorance, misguidance, and wrongful teaching. Open your mind to the secret.

Before you finish the first chapter, I hope you are set ablaze with the fires of desire for God's presence in a deeper way than you have ever experienced.

I have written this book in the form of an allegory, several short stories, and a teaching handbook. The mini-novels are all based on true testimonies. They have been enhanced and embellished, and fictional characters have been used to protect the innocent.

If you dare to join this revolution of worshipers, you will never again be satisfied with the status quo or with the hum-drum of Christianity. Religiosity will leave you with a bad taste. Instead, you will burn with the flames of integrity, Godly character, and passion for His presence. You will burn with the desire to do whatever it takes to move into the glory of God.

Read on and discover the dark secret pervading in the lives of many believers, and open your heart to discover the secret of God's heart.

Dr. Thomas Michael

ONE

The Secret

❦

The Secret

"Shhh, I hear something. Can you hear it? It's not music. It's more like whispers, perhaps, more like a hiss."

Something surreptitious lurks about in many believers' lives. You cannot see it, smell it, or touch it; but at times, you can feel it. Its presence is very real.

It clings to its victims like undetected mildew growing in an otherwise disinfected, immaculate kitchen. From the moment they awaken...

At twilight...

At dawn...

At dusk, it is there.

It secretly follows them when they lay their head down

to sleep, romps around in their dreams, and declares a false victory when their dreams turn to nightmares.

If you are trapped in its web of delusion, it is present every time you pray.

It is present when you lift your voice in worship to God.

It is there in the holiness of a beautifully anointed worship service.

"What is it?"

Shhh,

it's a secret.

It is a mystery, and mysteries must be discovered. Read closely, and you will discover **The Secret.**

In the New Testament, God's plans are often referred to as "mysteries". The English word mystery is a transliteration of the Greek word *musterion*, which means a sacred secret - something concealed that can be revealed.

There are different kinds of mysteries or secrets found in the New Testament: the mystery of Israel, the mystery of iniquity, the mystery of marriage, and the mystery of the Church.

As sure as there are Godly mysteries hidden in the light of God's glory, there are also mysteries cloaked in the darkness of evil. I am afraid it is not the kind of secret you anxiously long to repeat; and yet, its scandalous enigma must be unveiled and revealed.

What is a secret? The dictionary defines it: to set apart, kept from public knowledge or from the knowledge of a certain person or persons. The general term implies a concealing or keeping from the knowledge of others for any particular reason.

There is a clandestine, covert operation happening in churches all over the world. It has a greater consequence than stealing, fornicating, or even, murdering. This secret deed is not dealt with too often, perhaps, because it is not visible. It masquerades itself behind a smile, a friendly hug, even behind false humility.

It is not like the obvious sins of the flesh Christians so readily identify with backsliders and heathens. This sin has no visible consequence as do smoking, drinking, or sexual immorality. These sins have evidential, damaging effects on the one committing the act. A young lady sleeps with a boy: the eventual consequence is an unwanted and untimely pregnancy. A person who smokes accepts the risks of cancer. Still, none of these sins carry the eternal, consequential repercussions as **The Secret.**

There will be Christian men and women occupying Heaven who have had problems with smoking, drinking, and even engaging in sexual sins. However, there is one certainty; no one concealing **The Secret** will make Heaven his or her final residence!

This secret has been amidst the human race since the beginning of time. You can trace its existence all the way back before Adam and Eve.

There is no greater danger for believers than to fall prey to its fatal enticement.

It promises satisfaction and claims to avenge you with your enemies. It provides a temporal justification for your actions and emotions. The consequences of believing its lies can become caustic.

The Secret knows no boundaries and regards nothing dear nor sacred.

This dark secret finds its origin in a place far far away. Despite its short-lived moment in the annals of time, this secret paradoxically arose amidst a delightful place where everything to this day remains in perfect, sublime order. It is a place where one has never seen such beauty, opulence, and grandeur.

Amidst majestic mountains, vast seas, peaceful rivers, and sumptuous, rolling hills; nestled among a fortress of warriors protecting its timeless beauty stands...

A mighty Kingdom...

An imperial fortress...

A grand empire.

It is a Kingdom where everyone flows together in agreement for one purpose, one thought, and one goal.

A Kingdom where there are no disputes, no arguments, no jealousies, and absolutely no bitterness.

It is not a typical Kingdom.

The silence is impenetrable, yet, the sounds are unfathomable.

There is no darkness, only light - bright light beyond the scope of sun, moon, and stars.

In this Kingdom, there are many castles.

It is surrounded by a fortress built with a substance stronger than stone. It is protected by an impenetrable host of angelic beings. The gates to the entrance of the grandest kingdoms on earth pale in comparison to the magnificent, iridescent, white gates of this Kingdom. One look and you are smitten with speechless awe. If you dare look beyond these magnificent gates, you will never turn back. Your gaze will immediately, forever freeze upon an intoxicatingly glorious light.

In this Kingdom, there are three Kings who all reign together in supreme power.

All things work together for the good of the Kingdom.

***

In the following Chapter, you will be translated into another place, another time. You are about to enter the Kingdom of the Godhead, a place where the focus is and always has been **Worship**.

To properly set the atmosphere for what you are about to read, may I suggest you put on your favorite worship cassette or CD? (Preferably one of my CDs if you own one.) Let it play softly in the background as you read. I promise; you will not be disappointed.

Although I have written the scenes from the Kingdom in an allegoric format, the statements made are more than just an expression of creative ideas. They are revelations I have received during my time of worship. They are inspired by moments in the glory and a God-given creative mind. These ideas of the Kingdom of Heaven, surely, pale in comparison to the true beauty and majesty of Heaven. I pray that you are inspired; pushed to believe in a Heaven bigger, brighter, and more glorious than anything you have ever been taught, read about, or imagined.

This book has not been written in the conventional style of Christian teaching books. I have invested thousands of hours into the verbiage used in an attempt to captivate you, my reader, and draw you closer to the truth about some hidden secrets that may be costing you greatly.

I urge you to move into another level of worship with the Almighty and discover the secrets of His presence. It is in the depth of my worship that special moments have been forged into a revelatory teaching upon which the thesis for this story is founded.

***

And now, let us travel far above earth's atmosphere into galaxies known only to the Godhead.

Some exciting news has caused quite a stir among the angels from the western part of the Kingdom.

***

Instruments creating music...beautiful instrumental music...
"I want to sing, but my words are few."
Like a dream...
Like a vision...
"We're flying...we're soaring now...hold on."
Up...
Up even higher...
"Hold your breath..."
Whoosh!

"My clothes are flapping in the wind. It is like a vortex tunnel; I am surrounded by thick, crisp air."
Wind...lots of wind...
Strong winds...
A blur of lights all around...
Gales of wind blowing...
"We're soaring now. Oh my God, I have always wanted to fly. So, this is what it feels like to fly!"
Swoosh!
More wind...cold air...
Brightest light!
Whoosh!
Flying higher...higher...higher...higher

Blackout!

"Hold on; I think we've broken through earth's atmosphere. The Kingdom is just ahead."

Cold, ice cold, but not uncomfortable or painful like being lost in some snowcapped mountain forest.
Unbelievable beauty...
Colors - radiant light...brighter than the sun...

"I hear something...in the distance...sounds I've never heard before...the most beautiful chanting sounds."
Holy, holy, holy...
"Wait."
"What is that?"
"Look down...don't be afraid. That's the most beautiful, shiny gold I have ever seen! It is radiant; it's like you can see through it. It feels like thick water. Try it! Grab some, and throw it up in the air."
Sparkles falling...

"Look! To the left is a magnificent mountain taller than any mountain I have ever seen or than any man has ever climbed. And over there on the other side of the streets of gold, is that the most splendid river flowing with the bluest, crystal-clear water you have ever seen? Look how the water moves so rapidly; and yet, it remains undisturbed. It moves so perfectly in rhythm that it looks like a glass mirror."

Splendor...
Majesty...
Beauty...
Ultimate Glory...

Speechless.

TWO

The Birth of Music

Scene I
The Birth of Music

The stage was set.

The players had been assigned by the Godhead.

The Godhead emerged from their Secret Place known to all in the Kingdom as the Holy Chambers. It was made of the purest gilded gold. The walls were ornately covered with every stone imaginable and some too distinctly beautiful to imagine. It was busily beauteous but not ostentatious.

The furnishings were of the grandest proportions and still did not seem to fill the holy space.

The Holy Chambers had windows that climbed and

climbed till their end was not visible. They were draped with deep amethyst colored drapes trimmed in a gold bullion fringe. The sheers were made of finely woven silver mesh with beautifully designed gold inlaid crowns. The silver mesh was more like liquid silver, for it flowed with the Heavenly breeze like gossamer wings.

The Divine Three were settled into Their thrones. Their hearts raced with anticipation of what the angels had been rustling about for ages. In the Kingdom of the Holy Beings, one day is like a thousand years, and a thousand years is like one day.

The backdrop was the seventh Heaven where the throne room is located.

The stage was the Mount of the Congregation on the north side of the Kingdom.

All the angels were positioned for the event of the dawn; it would be the concert of the ages.

The Holy One had designed, adorned, and bestowed musical abilities upon a unique angel that rivaled the songs the Morning Stars had sung for epochs and eons.

This angel would sing the song of Heaven. A song so beautiful and so holy, only the Godhead knew of its existence. It was written, scripted, and orchestrated by the masterful creativity of the one and only Holy Ghost, or Holy One as everyone in Heaven refers to Him.

It was a song of pure, diamond clear worship...

A song of glory...

A song of splendor...

A song of majesty...

A song of power...

The light bearer, son of the morning, was arrayed like no other. He was magnificently and marvelously formed and fashioned strictly for the song of Heaven. His name was Lucifer, Angel of Light. You have never seen an angel like this one.

Out of his ebony eyes glowed a light so bright, it burned like fire. His hair was a deep raven black that flowed with soft waves down the middle of his broad back. His matching eyebrows arched with a perfect arch that set off his penetratingly deep-set, intense eyes. His physique was bold, strong, and masculine with a delicate touch of tenderness that made him femininely attractive.

The Godhead had agreed on the highest mountain in all of Heaven, the beautiful Mount of the Congregation, as the meeting ground for the worship concert.

Lucifer did not have to rehearse or learn the song of Heaven, for it was in him already. He was music in visible form.

All the stars, planets, and galaxies had gathered for the great, epic masterpiece of worship; a musical virtu of honour, glory, and majesty to the Godhead.

Never before had so much emphasis been placed on one activity in the Kingdom. This was the all-time event. Could there ever be anything more spectacular, more regal than this monumental affair of worship?

The Almighty sat proudly on His throne arrayed in all His splendor. His Spirit soared at the anticipation of this imperious event.

He was decorated by angels encircling Him as though they were gliding on the beautiful spectrum of colors that formed a perfect rainbow around His omnipotent presence.

His face shone with the splendor of the entire Kingdom. His eyes were like blazing fire full of compassion. His hair was stark white and ethereally flowed like gossamer wings that seemingly billowed out and formed the clouds that surrounded Him. He had a strong, masculine, gorgeous face with an ever-etched somber smile that dominated His beautiful countenance. To look upon His beauty was more than I could stand. I was drawn in by His soothing eyes of love; and yet, they cut straight to my heart.

His was the honour forever and ever...

Just when the angels thought they had reached forever, everything would begin again as though it had been the first time. Nothing ever aged nor grew tiresome; it was always afresh and anew in this beyond imagination Kingdom.

The chants the angels had chanted for billions of years were as pristine as the first time ever they uttered the first notes of existence.

It was not that the Almighty had grown tired of their worship. His existence was verified by their worship, and Heaven would not be Heaven without it. But now, Lucifer, the son of the morning would create sounds never before uttered or heard. The Almighty had put forth His very best in shaping and designing this creature of worship.

The Son of Glory sat upon His throne dressed in royal regalia. He, too, had angels encircling Him. They created a unique sound with the smooth susurrations of their robes flapping in the stillness of the celestial air that filled the place of His presence. These angels created their own circle that connected with the circle of angels surrounding the Almighty and the Holy One, creating a link effect - three circles interconnected.

The Son of Glory was more brilliant than the sun and the stars melded together and ignited by flames. His face resembled the Almighty's with long glistening golden hair that cascaded over His shoulders. It framed the handsomeness of His magnificent face with an eccentricity that remained reverently holy. His eyes were not like that of a human, a single color with striations in a darker shade. Within each orb, there was a collection of turquoise-blue and silver-blue accented with cobalt. The pattern of striations was formed by the alternations of these three dazzling pigments: each one a jewel in their own right. They were eyes full of mystery and wonder, piercingly all-knowing. His stare was mesmerizing.

When I finally moved my gaze from the Almighty, I looked into the eyes of the Son of Glory, and I could see myself in Him. It was as though I was Him, and He was me. I cannot explain it. His eyes carried and portrayed what I felt deep inside of me. They told of things no one knew but me. Even things that I had forgotten were written in His beautiful eyes. I began to weep. And just as I felt a tear trickle down my cheek, there was a tear moving down His cheek perfectly reflecting my tear. It was like looking into a mirror; only, His beautiful face was my face.

His was the glory forever and ever...

I wiped my eyes, and when I finally looked up, I was facing in the direction where the Holy One hovered. He flanked the left side of the emerald throne. He was gentle, pure, and within Him were contained the vaults of all knowledge. He was transparent as a crystal sea; He hovered over His throne waiting for action. He gleamed as the glory of the Son radiated upon His vesture.

On Him rested Wisdom. She was His robe and covered Him from top to bottom. She wrapped her arms around Him and clung to Him so intimately; she was engrafted to Him. She rested softly upon His shoulders, and He became her sanctity. Her beauty was radiant like shimmering, transparent mother of pearl. She only supplemented His beauty and not in a competitive manner; she simply complimented Him.

His face was so sinlessly pure and holy with dazzlingly green eyes similar to multifaceted emeralds. They sparkled, radiating a mystical blend of rainbow colors. These colors splashed on me and pierced right through my heart. As they danced around, in, and through me; I felt pain, not like the pain we associate with abrasions and contusions upon our skin. Instead, it was like a sharp electrical stinging that became a necessity to my existence, and I welcomed it. It charged my body like a fibrillator resuscitates the heart of a victim suffering a heart attack.

No human face could match His translucent, handsome visage. It was framed by a full head of long silver hair, a mane that wafted away from His face by a specially assigned pneumatic breeze that honourably fulfilled its purpose.

His was the power forever and ever!

To the Godhead belong honour, glory, and power forever and ever, world without end!

All mighty, all powerful, all knowing; the Three agreed on every action, every thought, every word; They were One.
One God...
One Lord...
One Spirit...
One Omnipotent Supreme Super-Power!

***

In the distance, trumpets sounded.

Cornets, horns of every size, and horns uniquely shaped resounded with mighty peals of psaltery and praise announcing the arrival of God's most recent creation. Each layer of trumpets from the far side of the Kingdom could be heard louder and louder as they signaled one to another. They sounded from every direction of the great Kingdom.

Like a domino effect, they played in thunderous crescendos.

From miles away, the music echoed filling the four corners of the Kingdom with triumphal music. One after the other, they heralded the arrival of the Kingdom's first worship leader.

And just when one would think the trumpets had produced the perfect sounds of proclamation, Gabriel appeared!

He blew the blast of his instrument, a matchless sound unique to its revolutionary design.

His instrument was made of the purest silver and extended far beyond his arms length. Its shape was like a trumpet but had multiple flutes that sounded in harmonic intervals with every blast. It played multiple notes simultaneously. It sounded like all the trumpets melded together creating one blast, one sound that could not be comprehended with mere hearing for it was supernatural.

It was gentle, yet, powerful...

Loud, yet, soft...

Fearsome, yet, comforting...

It echoed and reverberated throughout the Kingdom and expanded the Heavens as it blew through the layers of clouds that had been situated since the beginning of beginnings. Change was in the atmosphere and spawned excitement and joy. Angels danced in circles up and down the streets of transparent gold. They spiraled around and around in triumphal halals.

***

The newest member of the upper echelon of Heaven arrived in splendor and majesty, arrayed with beauty beyond what I could imagine.

The wonderment of his presence caused a rustling among the cherubs. They oohed and awed and paled in the light of the being's splendor.

He climbed higher and higher to the peak of the mount. He spread his four wings to their fullest, covering the entire mountaintop.

Suddenly, Michael, the archangel appeared out of nowhere and with the mighty flapping of his wings positioned himself on one side of the mount. He stood at attention as would a guard watching over the crown jewels of a monarchy. He spread one of his wings toward Lucifer's and connected with it while the other came across the front of the mount.

The third of the hierarchical beings, Gabriel, appeared before the throne and laid his instrument of worship at the feet of the Godhead. He beamed his way to the opposite side of the mount and connected his wings with Michael and Lucifer's. A perfect triangle was created, and the concert was about to begin.

Lucifer faced the north side of the Kingdom because that is where the Godhead positioned Their marvelous thrones. Two of Lucifer's wings extended over his head in the direction of the thrones; the other two extended out from his broad back toward Michael and Gabriel.

***

The Almighty's throne was made of the deepest green emerald stone one has ever imagined. Its color was rich and deep, yet, transparent as glass. Facets were etched and carved into every fraction of the throne. Each one prismatically cast a myriad of light that pierced through the clouds creating a burst of rays trajecting down to the atmospheres far below into worlds unknown; worlds yet to be created.

The Son of Glory's throne was made of the deepest

blood-red stone. It was hewn out of one mammoth ruby. There were no joints or parts; it was simply one precious gem. Its facets were cut, etched, and carved like the Almighty's but with finer, more delicate intricacies. Again, a kaleidoscope of colors exploded bursting out in all directions intertwining with the Almighty's.

The throne of the Holy One was made of a perfect, unblemished diamond. It was like no diamond one has ever seen, for it was not produced by the intense heat of years and years of wear and pressure on a single piece of coal. This diamond had never known the maltreatment and darkness of coal. It had always been pure; it had always been pristinely clear.

Perfectly symmetrical patterns were cut deep into its surface like the finest, purest crystal. These etchings did not have the freestyle form that the Son of Glory's had. They were in perfect, concise order. Their precise laconic cuts were a part of a master design and not simply cut to fill space.

The Holy One was passionate about order and sequence. He had seen to every detail of the concert. His joy was made perfect when everything was executed with excellence. He is excellence personified.

The brightness of the diamond prisms intertwined with the ruby red from the Son of Glory's throne, along with the deep emerald of the Almighty's, created a rainbow of multihued colors beyond imagination.

Around the throne were billions of finely cut prisms hanging like icicles suspended in the air by their sheer will to adorn the throne room. They served no special purpose. They simply fashioned a backdrop, a curtain of dramatic splendor for the Godhead.

Each prism was so fixedly and intensely bright; they did not simply cast light but created their own compositions as they ricocheted off one another. The lights danced around the throne as though each had its own personality and existence. They spun in circles, never breaking out of their perfectly aligned rows. It is not that a string of some sort held them in their vertical lines; they simply adhered to the order of the Kingdom.

The angels had never before seen the throne assembly room. No created being had ever been on this side of the mount. This was reserved for the Godhead alone. Not that it had been a forbidden area; on the contrary, it simply served as a differentiating factor between the everlasting Godhead and the created beings of Heaven.

The angels had been restrained for ages and ages by an unseen shield of light that was so bright, mere eyes could not comprehend it. Its presence was known only by a *knowing*.

The entire Heavenly host, the cherubim, seraphim, and the four living creatures directed their monotonous worship toward Lucifer.

The concert was now under way.

The magnificent angel of light had been designed with multiple instruments of worship built into his person. He was like an entire orchestra, and his music sounded like a symphonic fantasia.

He stood at the summit of the mount singing the overtures of love and worship. The music soared above the skies and beneath. It danced around the thrones as it echoed from the valley below and filled the great hall.

Angels hovered over the entire mountain. Ten thousand times ten thousand angels voiced the sounds of Heaven giving birth to the song of worship. Verbiage never before used was added to the lexicography of Heaven.

Every word, every note, every breath was filtered through Lucifer. He took the glory of the music, mingled it with fire, and presented it before the thrones of the Godhead. And They were pleased...

They were honoured...

They were magnified.

The Almighty, the Son of Glory, and the Holy One stood in honour of the song. It was a familiar song from deep within Them that had come full circle.

Worship was virtue from the Godhead spilled out and released upon the angels to provide them with a God-like image, giving them access to become intimate with the Godhead.

Essentially, the Godhead worshiped Themselves as Their virtue was returned in a combination of fire and music morphed into worship from within Their own personage.

And it fell upon Them like a liquid garment of the purest silk.

The holy fire of worship did not burn; instead, it caused the Almighty to shine brighter.

The eyes of the Son of Glory radiated more brilliantly with luminous fire.

And the Holy One became more transparent as the symphonies crescendoed and magnified the Godhead.

Lucifer opened his mouth, and music was visibly voluble and flowed out of him. He lifted his hands, and the music became louder and modulated higher and higher.

Andante!
Allegro!
Fortissimo!

The music soared reaching up, reaching out, and reaching within.

The hanging prisms swayed rhythmically with each note.

The angels opened their mouths in cadenced unison, and Lucifer fashioned the song of Heaven.

Never before had worship ascended to such heights of glory. The chanting of angels had been transformed! Their metrical chants, previously, had only filled the present Heaven where they stood. Now, the worship took flight. It soared through all the Heavens and filled each level with honour, glory, and power.

Music flowed like sheer, iridescent liquid bound by no gravity and blanketed all of Heaven. It cast a hazy glow on every flicker of light.

The four living creatures held their eyes fixed on the instrument of worship. They watched his every move and copied him as they cried, "Holy, holy, holy, Lord, God Almighty. Who was, Who is, and is to come."

The Heavenly host echoed their cries with their verse, "For thine is the Kingdom and the power and the glory forever and ever amen!" Not one voice out of sync, not one echo misplaced; the verses had been articulated for ages and ages and ages.

The song of Heaven was born in that very instant when the four living creatures joined the worship led by Lucifer.

It was a beautiful day, a monumental day in the Kingdom.

THREE

And Heaven Was Silent

And Heaven Was Silent

"And Heaven was silent. Michael and his angels fought against the dragon, and the dragon and his angels fought back. However, he was not strong enough, and they lost their place in Heaven." These first few words of the passage found in Revelation Chapter Twelve are somewhat disturbing.

Picture in your mind a scenario of Heaven: the pearly gates, the walls constructed of gemstones, and streets of pure gold.

Picture a Kingdom of majesty, honour, glory, and beauty with one objective: to provide worship to the Godhead.

In the midst of pure worship produced by angels for centuries, even millennia, around the eternal throne of God;

there arose an enigma: a dark, malevolent governance.

Long before there was a place called hell, before angels knew any other worlds existed, in the midst of the agreement that flowed among the ranks of Heaven; there arose a surreptitious *coup d' état.*

I have always envisioned everything being perfect, sublime, and orderly in Heaven; and it is. Still, amidst this sanctuary of holiness, a war took place; Lucifer and one-third of the angels waged war against the remaining angelic host. Lucifer and his minions were cast out of the Kingdom as a result of his rebellion. His rebellion transpired as a result of *the secret.*

Remember, a secret must be discovered. Keep reading, and you will soon crack the code, and the secret will be revealed. This mystery has been kept from you for a reason.

Most people are not aware that Lucifer was adorned as one of God's most beautiful creations. He is not the horned, red-tailed, pitchfork-carrying devil many perceive him to be.

Countless believers have a strong persuasion that Satan is at fault for the break-up of marriages, the cause of sickness, and many other sad maladies that have plagued mankind throughout the centuries.

I am amazed at how much blame has been placed on an impotent, fallen angel.

While writing this, I am sitting in a hotel in London. I am surrounded by countries that have been oppressed for centuries by demonic forces. And yet, there is a thriving, strong, and vibrant Church fully alive! Are these people under a heavier assault by demonic forces than we are? Europe has much more witchcraft, wizardry, and paranormal happenings than we as Americans have. Still, on any given day, you can turn on your television and hear message after message about the devil attacking this believer and that.

Could it be that we have misplaced our focus?

Could it be that we have been deceived into believing that Satan has the kind of power that could rival the presence of the Living God within us?

Are we crediting the devil with having equal power to the Almighty?

Oh Sister So-and-So or Brother So-and-So fell from grace. We need to rebuke the devil out of them...

This other person had an adulterous affair...

This one is on drugs...

This one is an alcoholic...

The Church has attributed all these human frailties to the devil's workings. ***I stand convinced; if you are a mature child of God, the devil does not have enough power to cause your soul to stray from God.***

There is a wonderful passage in the book of Isaiah that tells us, "No weapon formed against us shall prosper..." How many weapons are to prosper in your life? Not one!

No curse spoken against you can prosper; unless, you are in rebellion. Numbers 22:4 gives a detailed account of a man who unsuccessfully tried to curse the Israelites. Every time he tried to curse them, God would bless them instead.

Yet, so many in the Body of Christ complain about how the devil attacked them or how he has robbed them. They credit Satan with the power to bring deadly diseases upon their lives or the ability to make them stumble in their walk.

I have heard the passage; *The thief cometh not but for to kill, steal, and destroy,* quoted more times than any other Scripture. This has become the thesis for the idea that Satan is out to kill us. This passage is simply clarifying the difference between Christ, the true Shepherd and false, self-proclaimed messiahs.

Satan's expertise is deception - counterfeiting. He cannot harm you; he can simply attempt to deceive you. His forces can deceive you into making wrong choices that lead to wrong results.

Still, no weapon formed against you shall prosper!

How many weapons does the Scripture say will prosper in a child of God's life? None!

Why then, are the alleged weapons of divorce, alcoholism, fornication, lust, and many other evils prospering against God's people?

Why are Satan's fiery darts purportedly getting past the armor? Could it be among all the biblical confessions, prayers, and scriptural quoting something is invalidating the power of the Word?

It is the traditions of men that make the Word of God ineffective. Traditionally, Christians believe that Satan is at fault for every difficulty in their lives. There could be nothing further from the truth.

There is nothing more liberating than accepting the fact that much of what happens in life is based upon one's *choices.*

How sad! When God's people take the position of blindly accusing Satan for their faults. That is like implying that Satan got one over God.

The truth is Satan is a loser! His authority has no bearing upon a believer unless we invite him in.

The devil knows zero about heathen living. You will not find him in the crack house, the prostitute's house, or for that matter, the White House.

Satan's address is not somewhere in the middle of Las Vegas or on the notorious Bourbon Street of New Orleans.

I can see this huge, sacred golden calf rocking back and forth in your mind.

I believe traditions and mindsets are the cause of the ineffectiveness of the Word of God in Christians' lives. We must undo the traditions of men and religiosity that keep so many from breaking through to the blessed life.

Your break through is not based on defeating Satan; it is based on your willingness to do things God's way. Satan was already defeated at Calvary. If you are waiting for a break through contingent upon your emotions, you may have to wait a long while.

There will be times you will not feel anything; it will have to do with a *knowing*.

There is a desperate need for people to serve the Lord based on their knowledge of the Word and not by emotions only. One of the biggest secrets in the Kingdom of God is that many are deceived and do not know it. Still, the Bible reassures that the knowledge of the glory of the Lord shall fill the earth. (Habakkuk 2:14)

There have been times when I have prophesied or given an interpretation to a message in tongues and had no feelings or emotions to accompany my actions.

God did not call us to walk a walk of feelings. He called us to walk the walk of trusting in His Word.

WISDOM PRINCIPLE: FAITH PRODUCES WHAT YOU WANT; TRUST PRODUCES WHAT GOD WANTS.

God's people must know what they know based on the Word and not on emotional experiences only.

God wants to bring His Church into a whole new dimension of knowledge, but this knowledge is released according to His glory. And His glory cannot be revealed amidst the workings of the flesh.

Allow me to iterate; Satan knows nothing about *heathen* living. He craves the worship, he once offered God.

The Heavenlies were originally divided into thirds. Michael, the archangel, led the warring angels. Gabriel, the chief messenger angel, governed a third of the angels; and finally, Lucifer, who was the chief worship leader or choir director, was over the remaining host.

I understand this may appear as a controversial thought.

You may refer to theologians, your Bible, and commentaries and argue my point. However, I believe, upon the expulsion of the worship leader and his followers, the worship section was removed. Thus, **Heaven became silent.**

This book is not a deliberation on the topic of Satan's existence and power, rather, on his deeds. It is about where he works and where he has been given permission to work.

Prior to the removal of Lucifer and his fallen angels, Heaven's worship was perfect; it flowed in faultless harmony. There was no dissonance or chaos among the perfectly orchestrated worship of Heaven. Then, Lucifer became jealous of the worship offered to Jehovah. While he created and directed the great Heavenly concertos, God received all the glory. Lucifer's jealousy resulted in offense, and his offense evolved into stubborn pride. Lucifer got his feelings hurt because he got no recognition for his contribution to the music of Heaven.

The perfect song of the Spirit became defiled, polluted, and tainted with motives of jealousy, envy, and offense resulting in pride. Music underwent a dramatic metamorphic change. What was once holy and reserved for the faultless, pristine atmosphere of Heaven became polluted.

This sacred music was now turned over to the controls of a self-centered, self-serving fallen angel. Could it be that this was man's first introduction to music? Hence, we arrive at the ungodly music known to us today.

Could this be part of Satan's secret ambition? It was obvious that the Kingdom of Heaven was not penetrable to his dubious deeds.

Satan's true identity is cloaked in secrets, secrets, and more secrets.

Because of His unblemished, untarnished integrity, God would not allow Himself to remove the gift of song from Lucifer. Lucifer became *the lord of the music.*

The Scriptures do not support the theory of angels singing. Even in the climactic close of this age, it is the multitude of people who have been martyred who sing and not the angels.

The Book of Revelation sheds light on the fact that angels spoke or chanted their worship. "And all the angels stood round about the throne, and about the elders and the four beasts, and fell before the throne on their faces, and worshiped God, *saying,* Amen: Blessing, and glory, and wisdom, and thanksgiving, and honour, and power, and might, be unto our God for ever and ever. Amen." (Revelation 7:11,12) The angels John saw in his vision were not singing; it is recorded they were merely declaring words of adoration.

The word *saying* comes from a Greek word, which means: to relate in words usually of systematic or a set discourse; an individual expression or speech respectively; to break silence. They speak with rhythmic patterns creating sounds that resemble chanting.

Angels carry messages and herald reports, but they do not sing. It is quite apparent there is a great need for worshipers since the fall of Lucifer. This is why I believe *worship is the desperate cry of man's soul reaching up for its Creator.*

Music had to undergo a cleansing before it could again be suitable to God's standards. It had to be free from jealousy, envy, offense, and pride.

Music in and of itself cannot be classified as evil; moreover, the vessel who sings it or the lyrical content is what contaminates it.

Some singers appearing on television and churches all over the country lack anointing. Not because the song they sing is not anointed, rather, their vessel is not pure. They are harboring offenses that have not been dealt with. They are harboring the secret power of lawlessness and may very well be completely unaware.

All music originates from God.

One of Satan's secrets is diverting Christians' attention

to believe that only secular or worldly music can be satanic.

Secular music is secular music. It was never designed to glorify God and, therefore, cannot be constituted as satanic; it is simply carnal.

What is satanic music?

A person with offense in his heart singing a worship song is no different than Lucifer sitting in the holiness of Heaven singing his worship song with evil in his heart. This is where satanic music was born. Attempting to offer worship to God with offense in the heart is equal to Satan's polluted worship.

Secular music feeds the flesh. It can stir up emotions that may influence you to make wrong choices. Much like secular music, praise also stirs up emotions. There is nothing wrong with emotions; it is what you do with those emotions that counts.

The emotional effects of praise often times cause us to focus on our own feelings and not on the feelings of the one we are praising. Thus, it is important to recognize that praise is the key to enter into the temple courts but worship is the vehicle that takes us beyond the veil.

True worship can never be satanic because it must originate from a pure heart.

"Who shall ascend into the hill of the Lord? Or who shall stand in His holy place? He that hath *clean hands*, and a *pure heart;* who hath not lifted up his soul unto vanity, nor sworn deceitfully." (Psalm 24:3,4 italics added)

Worship is not a part of the service that everyone moves into. Everyone may participate in the praise, but only those with a pure heart and holy hands can put on the garments of intimacy. It is these garments that cover our own nature and present us to the King of Kings for intimate relationship.

WISDOM PRINCIPLE: WORSHIP IS THE SEED OF INTIMACY THAT PRODUCES THE UNIMAGINABLE.

Matthew 18:19, the antithesis to offense, compares the power of agreement with music. In the Amplified Bible to *agree* means: to harmonize together, make a symphony together. Thus, agreement is true worship, making melody in our hearts to the Lord. "And be not drunk with wine, wherein is excess; but be filled with the Spirit; Speaking to yourselves in psalms and hymns and spiritual songs, singing and making melody in your heart to the Lord." (Ephesians 5:18,19) Spirit-filled living is simply walking in peace with your fellow brethren; keeping free from strife, bitterness, envy, and offense (with music in your heart).

Most believers strive to live peaceably with their neighbor but end up losing their joy in their striving. It is the attitude of worship that keeps us singing, even while others are at odds with us.

Agreement takes us to a deeper level than unity. Unity implies we all must sing the same note in unison. Agreement gives the picture of everyone singing their own note in pure harmony with one another.

You cannot be offended at someone and sing melodies in your heart to the Lord. Offense robs its victim from the true joy of the Lord.

The Bible says Lucifer, the angel of worship, adorned the throne of God, and there was music in him. The song of Heaven was deep within his being.

I am a musician, and I love to sing and play the piano, but I have to *make* music with my instrument. Lucifer did not make music; he *was* music. Although I can give birth to notes with my voice, I can not harmonize alone. I must be in agreement with someone else's notes to create harmonies.

The purest form of worship is when we sing the song found deep within our spirits. It is the music of our souls that is transformed by the Spirit and presented as pure worship to God.

I envision Lucifer with the ability to raise an arm, and a chord rings out. Perhaps, when he stretches his wings, a couple of other chords join in. Could it be, when he takes flight, it is like the crescendo of an entire symphony playing in harmony? Maybe, when he raises his legs, the chords change. To say he is unique in God's creation would be an understatement.

Music and worship obviously play a large role in the atmosphere of Heaven.

Scientists have discovered and proven that the Aurora Borealis also known as the northern lights make sounds. They make music!

Scripture states that the morning stars have been singing for ages.

Lucifer was known as the angel of light. In view of these facts, it stands to reason that light is sound. Satan understands sound and may have more knowledge on the subject of music than anyone else.

His passion lies in diverting the attention of the Church to issues completely irrelevant to his assumed diabolical nature. That is where Satan feels most comfortable, in the midst of secrecy.

WISDOM PRINCIPLE: ANYTHING CLOAKED IN SECRECY HAS THE POTENTIAL OF BECOMING EVIL.

A young wife finds herself cloaked in the mantle of deep dark secrets that spiral her into a pit she scarcely escapes.

Marla had every right to be offended and bitter for what her husband did to her. The secrets he concealed became the open door to the darkest evil Marla would ever experience. Interestingly enough, the evil she experienced was a wake up call from God Himself. The demonic attack she thought she was under was actually God purging her motives. He thrust her into a nightmare that would reveal the wiles of harboring an offense.

***

...Kingdom Report...

Back at the Kingdom, the music continues as Lucifer leads the angelic host. They chant and worship for ages at a time, and he continues to filter the worship creating the most beautiful sounds ever heard.

Stay tuned for further updates.

Wait...
One moment please...

An update has just come through.

This is top-secret information coming from sources within the Kingdom. Something has happened to the music. More news to come later.

The Nightmare

❧

The Nightmare

I was a happily married woman with six beautiful children. If it had not been for the obstetrician who practically insisted on tying my tubes, I would have been perpetually pregnant.

Eric wanted as many children as the good Lord would bless us with. Of course, he was not the one giving birth to them and vomiting day after day.

One of my children had almost killed me; he weighed 13 pounds 10 ounces.

When little Teddy was older, he asked to see infant pictures of himself.

"I want to see baby pictures of me, mommy. Like the ones you have of baby Stephanie," he cried.

I said, "Sweetheart, these are your infant pictures."

He was sure that I loved the other children more than him because I had newborn pictures of them all and only toddler pictures of him. Little did he know that the assumed toddler pictures were his infant pictures.

My children were my joy.

I wasn't fulfilled much as a wife, but I gained strength from my relationship with Jesus Christ. I had accepted Christ as my Savior at a young age.

People knew me for my kind, loving, and forgiving spirit. I characterized myself as a Godly wife, since I had been married to my unsaved husband for many years; and still, I remained faithful to the ubiquitous turbulent marriage. It seemed I could not escape its embrace.

No matter how hard I tried, how much I prayed, it appeared that nothing ever changed my humdrum life. I was diligent in praying for my husband's conversion, trusting someday he would reward me with my greatest victory and become a believer.

It appeared nothing good, bad, or otherwise ever happened to me. Little did I know that one of my greatest victories would be the saving of my own soul and sanity.

My husband had always been domineering and quite demanding, but the one thing I never allowed him to do was deprive me from going to church.

My husband and I had many arguments over the years about attending church; and there were times, he physically tried to stop me. But when I believe in something, I always stand for it regardless of the consequences.

The way I see the Bible, it's either black or it's white; there are no gray areas.

Twenty years after the incident, I still remember the sordid details.

I was quite ill at the time; my health was not at its optimum, but I always tried to keep a positive attitude knowing that God was with me.

I had grown accustomed to reciting Scriptures to get me through tough times. One of my favorites was, "The Lord God will help me, therefore shall I not be confounded, therefore have I set my face like a flint and I know that I shall not be ashamed." I never felt shamed or disgraced, even when my husband was physically violent with me because I knew who I was in Christ.

My sister heard an evangelist, whom I respected and whose ministry I supported, was coming to town. I felt prompted to attend that evening's service. I thought, perhaps, I might receive a healing from the painful condition I had been suffering with. The doctors had diagnosed cancerous tumors in my abdomen that would be fatal unless I received a miracle. I was reluctant at first, but later, was thankful I had made the effort; God rewarded me with a miraculous healing.

I was so excited on the way home. My sister and I recounted over and over the wonderful things that had transpired in the service that evening. The way Brother Sidlow had called me out through a word of knowledge, my apprehension to go forward for fear he was not referring to me, and the sensation I had as I was healed.

Of course, he had to point me out all the way in the back where we were standing because I couldn't believe he was talking to me.

He called out for the lady in the orange and brown shawl with the big hairdo. I made my way to the front, and they ushered me onto the massive stage. The evangelist seemed so small from a distance; and now, he was bigger than life. My mouth was dry and my knees felt weak.

"The Lord shows me..." he spoke with his raspy, somewhat insensitive voice.

"I am healing the tumors in your abdomen. I, the Lord,

am able to touch your infirmities and make you whole."

My knees finally gave out, and I fell to the floor. At this point, I had no qualms as I had experienced earlier about falling down in front of the huge, excited, faith-filled crowd.

People began applauding and shouting praises to God. I continued to cry and knew that something had taken place inside of me. I knew I was healed.

When I reached my house after the service, what awaited me would prove to be the greatest test of forgiveness.

I had always considered myself a good Christian with good moral and ethical standards. I was a virgin when I married and expected my husband would have the same moral convictions as myself.

Years into our marriage, I learned of his indiscretions with other women when he frequented his favorite bars and nightclubs.

But what was I to do? Where could I go with six children?

I was forced to learn to cope with the shame and the pain and became skilled at putting up with my husband's extramarital affairs. I grew accustomed to forgiving him, consoling myself that at least he came home to me at the end of the day.

After all, I had read the second chapter of Malachi and was fully convinced that God hated divorce. So, divorce was out of the question.

Oh, there were many separations along the way, which helped me cope with my feelings and my occasionally confused emotions. I managed to keep them intact through my love for the Word of God.

Getting back to that horrible evening.

As I entered my house, my husband and next-door neighbor, Laura, were coming out of my bedroom. Laura looked right at me and giggled as she sashayed passed me. The glow in her piercing eyes divulged her silent, corrosive agenda.

You can imagine how I must have felt. I took a few steps backward until my back rested between the doorjamb and the wall. I froze and stood in complete silence. My heart sank, my hand went limp, and the purse I had clutched under my arm dropped to the floor. The thud reverberated in my dazed, confused mind.

No telling how long she had loomed her web of deception. No telling how long their odious affair had been going on.

I interrogated my husband until I gathered enough information to convince me of his injudicious behavior.

I thought I had mastered the art of forgiving my husband and was confident there was nothing he could do to make me lose my joy. I had forgiven him so many times before.

How? It is something that eludes me to this day. It must have been the power of God's Word working in me.

The Holy Spirit spoke softly, "Forgive them both." I had planned to forgive my husband for what he had allegedly done.

Perhaps, my mind was negotiating ways to rationalize all the affairs I speculated he had indulged in.

Perhaps, I had found a way to persuade myself that he really had done nothing wrong because I had never actually caught him in the act. But now, here it was blatantly thrown in my face. I found myself struggling to forgive the incident. I crumbled under the weight of the idea of being treated like such a fool. I don't think I have ever cried that much in my life.

Why was forgiveness different this time? Could it be that I had not really walked in true forgiveness with my husband's past? And would I be able to consider what had taken place a part of his past? At the moment, I could not think of anything but how I felt for myself. I had somehow learned to cope with the mess, and I was proud of myself for that.

But forgiveness was out of the question.

Again, the Holy Spirit prompted, "Forgive them both."

Why was forgiveness such a big deal now?

Why couldn't I just deal with the matter as I had successfully done so in the past?

I went about my usual routine, caring for my children, preparing the full course meal. Standing at the stove, stirring the pot, I daydreamed of a better life for me and my children. I could hear them laughing and playing in the background. The delicious aroma rising from the stew moved about me but had no enticement. My appetite had fled along with Laura as she walked past me.

My husband sat at the table unmoved by my tears and unaffected by my demure disposition.

I went to bed angry. I pulled the covers up over my head as though I were covering myself from an impending danger. Oh, how I wished it were all a bad nightmare that I could awaken from.

I mumbled softly directing my response to God, "I will not forgive them."

Once more, the Holy Spirit gently said, "Forgive them both." I rolled over in bed and felt my husband's leg rub against mine. I jerked away and muttered, "I'll never forgive you." I ignored the promptings and fell asleep.

My husband reached over and caressed my back. He pleaded with me to forgive him, but I was too angry to even consider it.

The next morning, I awoke thinking last night had only been an awful nightmare. Surely, this was all a horrible dream.

My mind quickly flashed back to the events of the day and the insolent look in Laura's eyes. A cold chill ran through my body causing me to shudder followed by a hot flash.

I was awakened by an excruciating pain in my chest. I felt I was dying. I thought to myself, "God healed me of cancer yesterday, but today, I will die from a heart attack."

I heard a voice audibly say, "Curse the Holy Spirit." It was a tormenting voice that would send cold chills through my aching body.

I was held captive by an oppressive weight that confined me to my bed. The freedom I had experienced the night before was now only a vague memory. I clamored for help from my children as they dressed themselves for school.

My husband had already left for the day, after having had a fitful sleep the night before, while I tossed and turned.

My oldest boy eventually called my parents and summoned them to my bedside. The prayers of my Godly parents that had seen me through many circumstances while still at home were now seemingly fruitless.

I remember pleading with God to forgive me for harboring an offense against my husband.

I never dreamed that unforgiveness would have such horrible consequences. I was sure God's forgiveness would be easily accessed when I was good and ready to deal with my anger.

After all, I felt justified in my rage and resentment, which I knew would last me until my grudge was satiated. I had forgiven him over and over; but this time, I wanted to feel vindicated. I wanted to make him feel some pain.

I knew the Scriptures warned against letting the sun go down on one's wrath, but I was in control, or so I thought. Besides, who really pays that much attention to these Scriptures?

My parents prayed for me hour after hour in shifts. I was terrified of being alone. I could not be left unaccompanied. This persisted for seven full days. I had only moments of rest; and then, I would doze off only to be awakened by the ghastly sight of a foreboding spirit hovering over me like a dark cloud constantly urging me to curse and blaspheme the Holy Spirit.

Where had these thoughts come from?

Why was I, a child of God, who had put Him first in my life; I, who had endured so much for the sake of the gospel, why was I going through this? I had grown up in church with higher values than anyone else I knew.

On the seventh day, a vision began to play out on a floating screen right before my eyes. I was cognizant and fully alert as the tormenting saga unfolded.

I was standing on the precipice of a steep cliff that had no bottom. The air was cold and damp and made my skin feel clammy. I could see it moving around on the foliage of the plant life; and yet, it was as though everything stood still. The plants had a green coloring; yet, appeared to have no life at all. They had an artificial appearance.

In the sky above, dark clouds hovered low. The wind howled; and in the distance, a lonely whippoorwill cried, and its sound echoed through the canyon far below.

It was a dark abyss with no end.

Even in my wildest imagination, I could never have come up with such a bone-chilling nightmare. I knew I had been placed there by something beyond my control.

I stood on the edge fearful of falling. As if out of nowhere, came a large fire-breathing dragon. He flapped his wings back and forth until he had perched himself next to me.

He was not the typical, mythological dragon portrayed by artists with a gruesome, gargoyle-looking face.

He had a wingspan that reached across the entire canyon where I had been placed. The luminosity of his eyes gave the impression that he could see from any direction. His voice had warm, inviting tones that were altered by dissonant sounds creating a far more gruesome sound than any horror show. It had a guttural, hissy sound and rang out from all four corners of the place where I was held captive.

The cry of the whippoorwill was drowned out by each gasp for air the dragon made. It was as though its every breath was laborious and toilsome. It was obvious that this beast had suffered some battle wounds in the past that had left him incapacitated. With each exhale, a hot lava-like fire would spew out of his mouth.

His feet resembled those of an eagle only they were mangled, twisted, and had the texture of the bark on a 100 year old oak tree. His tail was made of a thick, bark-like texture that twisted and coiled as though a snake had attached itself on the hind side of an eagle.

He snarled at me and hissed blowing wet, molten lava-like fire and billows of smoke in the direction where I was standing. The intense heat its presence created was stifling and made it difficult for me to breath. He hurled and swished his strong muscular tale, lashing out at me with vile accusations of blaspheme trying to push me over the edge.

Billows of smoke rolled in and out with every gasp for air he made. His exhalations created a dark fog mixed with the incandescence of the intense heat of his fire and cast an orange glow on the cliff.

At the end of the day, my episode with the dangers of unforgiveness finally came to a close. However, the unsavory saga was not complete until I had fully forgiven my husband, my neighbor, and myself.

Nine months later, I received a phone call from my neighbor; she was calling from the labor and delivery ward. She had given birth to a baby boy and made the comment that the baby looked much like my husband.

My willingness to walk in forgiveness and to remain in agreement with my marriage as well as my neighbor diminished the negative effects of her phone call. It was meant to inflict pain and foster bitterness; instead, it unlocked compassion within me.

I gave birth to two more children after Teddy and remained committed to my marriage. A few years later, Eric was diagnosed with cancer and gave his life to Christ while in the hospital, a year before he died. I was left alone to deal with six children on my own. I never resented him or begrudged him because I had placed my trust in God.

I had received healing in the very area that subdued my husband's life. God always vindicates His own, even, if it is at the very end.

***

WISDOM PRINCIPLE: OFFENSE SEEKS IMMEDIATE VINDICATION TO PROVE ITSELF CORRECT, WHILE AGREEMENT PATIENTLY ALLOWS GOD TIME TO VINDICATE.

The sad thing about avenging yourself is, you never feel vindicated nor satisfied. When God vindicates you, it is based on His holy wrath and not your carnal wrath.

It may seem incomprehensible to you to forgive such an offense. Forgiveness is not about simply forgiving the other person; it is about not allowing yourself to become trapped in the jungle of offense. And the only way out of this bug infested, swampy jungle is through the bridge of forgiveness.

You may try to hack your way through, thinking you are escaping the dangers of the jungle; but all too soon, you will end up in a pit of quicksand.

Unforgiveness is like a pit of quicksand. It will swallow you whole and suffocate the life out of you. Have you ever felt like your heart was coming through your throat when someone upset you? Unforgiveness strangles its prey like a python.

Use the bridge of forgiveness to get to the other side of offense and stay out of the quicksand!

FOUR

Forgiveness

Forgiveness

It has been said, "To err is human; to forgive is divine." Where does one acquire the kind of forgiveness to look beyond deep emotional hurts and the whole gamut of abuse?

The act of forgiveness is about giving. The words *for* and *give* in Webster's Dictionary mean (for): in place of and instead of - (give): to turn over the possession or control of to someone without exchange.

WISDOM PRINCIPLE: FORGIVENESS IS AN ACTION THAT DOES NOT CALL FOR RECIPROCATION; IT IS BASED ON YOUR WILLINGNESS TO GIVE CONTROL TO ANOTHER.

You give forgiveness in place of how you were wronged, regardless of what is owed to you.

David was a man filled with passion: passion for God's presence and unfortunately for his own flesh. His actions were often misinterpreted as harsh and self-seeking; and yet, he was known as a man after God's own heart. As contradicting and paradoxical as that may seem, God liked him. God was impressed with his passion for wisdom and worship.

David had reason to retaliate against King Saul, who at one time was like a father to him. Despite King Saul's rage and erratic behavior, David was *always* willing to *forgive*. Saul ordered his men to hunt David down like some animal. Still, David was quick to forgive, even his own son, Absalom who attempted to dethrone him.

There can only be one rationale behind David's ability to extend forgiveness. David was a worshiper. For many, forgiveness is a costly undertaking; but for David, there was no other option. He was passionate about every thing he did, even forgiving. David had grasped something that few have been able to understand. He was unwilling to compromise his time in the presence of the Lord.

A worshiper is an individual who is more concerned about his position with God than with men. **Worship creates a willingness in man to forgive any offense at any cost for the sake of abiding in God's presence.**

I consider myself to be a forgiving person, not because I have a meek and mild demeanor, but because I cherish my relationship with the Holy Spirit. Much like King David, I would not want to risk missing one moment in God's presence.

If you are harboring unforgiveness toward someone in your life, whether they are presently a part of your life or a part of your past, you must choose to forgive them for the sake of your relationship with the Lord. **No one's feelings toward you are worth missing one moment of fellowship with your**

Savior. And do not forget, He is the only One who can truly save you!

The secret erects its walls of seclusion around its victim, all the while isolating him or her from the freedom to love. I John 4:20 says, "If a man say, I love God, and hateth his brother, he is a liar: for he that loveth not his brother whom he hath seen, how can he love God whom he hath not seen?" It is impossible to love God while harboring unforgiveness.

Some of Christ's final words while on the cross were, "Father, forgive them, for they know not what they do." Could it be that the Messiah was placing a stronger emphasis on forgiveness than simply abstaining from offense? Jesus Himself said it was impossible that we not get offended.

Before long, each one of us will have to give up our struggle trying to be perfect with everyone around us and be forced to admit our human frailty. The fact is it is impossible to go one day without getting offended by something or someone. The second fact is, it is impossible to go one day without offending someone around us because we are human beings, and that is our nature. Naturally, that is no excuse to go around being offensive and disagreeable with everyone around you.

Jesus was sorely offended at His own disciples because of their lack of faith, their inability to comprehend what He was trying to tell them, and many other reasons. And yet, Jesus was the Master forgiver. There were times Jesus called them "vipers" and "you faithless bunch of hypocrites". People unnerved Christ on a regular basis, yet, He never missed one moment with His Heavenly Father.

The Pharisees and Sadducees upset Him to no end; and still, He forgave all. Only a loving Savior could forgive having been wrongfully accused, tried, and crucified.

What can we learn from our loving, forgiving Savior?

He was a Master at the art of forgiving. In other words, He was quick to lay down any type of resentment over human frailty.

He did not harbor unforgiveness against those who crucified Him; instead, He said, "Father, forgive them for they know not what they do."

We have studied and placed the importance on knowing the sins of *commission* for so long that we have failed to recognize the sins of *omission*.

The focus has been trying not to get offended, which is impossible, instead of learning to be quick to forgive. People omit the fact that everyone is an *equal opportunity offender* and should be an *equal opportunity forgiver* as well.

You are more like Christ when you are quick to forgive, rather than, when you pretend that you are never offended.

Oh, are you still wondering what the secret is?

Have you discovered it yet? Surely by now, you have seen a thread of resemblance between Lucifer's first offense and man's offense. Still, I am not going to let you in on the secret because you must discover it for yourself.

WISDOM PRINCIPLE: FORGIVENESS IS THE FRUIT OF THE GODLY.

Only those who walk in the Spirit can feast on the sweet, delicious nectar of forgiveness. To forgive is to be forgiven; what could be sweeter than that?

The Psalmist wrote, "O taste and see that the Lord He is good." God's goodness toward us is that He loved us while we were yet sinners. He forgave us all our debts. The goodness of the Lord for a fallen people is His merciful forgiveness.

The next time you think you cannot forgive someone, think about the goodness of the Lord in your life; He forgave you and died in your stead.

Forgiveness is often an absent, yet, vital element in the process of self-discipline.

The Scripture reveals there are two kinds of forgiveness: Divine Forgiveness and Human Forgiveness.

WISDOM PRINCIPLE: MAN'S ABILITY TO FORGIVE IS BASED ON MAN'S WILL, BUT GOD'S ABILITY TO FORGIVE IS BASED ON LOVE.

In the Old Testament, the word *forgive* is mentioned fifty times and is from the Hebrew word, *salach,* which means: to forgive, to pardon, to spare someone or to relieve someone of the burden of their offense. When Jesus spoke in the New Testament and said, "Your sins are forgiven," the Pharisees were taken aback because they were still under the old law when only God could forgive.

In Psalm 25:18, David cries out to the Lord and says, "Look upon mine affliction and my pain; and forgive all my sins." Here, the word *forgive* means: to accept, advance, arise, exalt, and to marry. God's forgiveness elevates us from our iniquitous, unworthy position and makes us eligible for marriage with God. His forgiveness is like a shaft of light shining into the obscurity of our wretchedness illuminating our downcast countenance.

A person who has been forgiven radiates the joy of the Lord.

In the New Testament, the word *forgive* means: to forgive, to cry, to forsake, lay aside, grant as a favor, gratuitously, in kindness, to free fully, and to relieve. Forgiveness gives the forgiven the freedom to be. A debt binds an individual and forgiveness fully relieves and frees the individual based on gratuitous giving.

Unforgiveness constricts the channel of communication and sanctification between God and the believer. You cannot say you are not offended if you are walking in unforgiveness. Likewise, you cannot say you are walking in forgiveness, yet, harboring offense.

In the book of Matthew, we read that the power to bind and loose was bestowed upon the believer. Unforgiveness has a binding effect on those who are offended. It is also dangerous to everyone who comes in contact with the offended.

Forgiving the offender is just as important as the offender making his or her heart right. An offended individual could decide he or she was wrong and ask for forgiveness from the ones they have hurt. Nevertheless, if the individual who was hurt refuses to release the offender, they have by default elected to bind that individual. What a potent agent of power has been placed in the hands of the believer. It can either be used for good or for evil.

Practice instant reconciliation. Read that again. Practice means to do something over and over until it becomes as natural as walking.

A few years ago, I endured the criticism of some people who were deeply offended and were harboring bitterness against me for things I had never done. I was very hurt and felt very betrayed. I remember practicing over and over in my spirit forgiving them, the day that I would finally see them again. It was over two years before I ran into them. I embraced them both and experienced what I had practiced over and over in my heart.

Choose to forgive quickly.

Walk in forgiveness daily.

In the eighteenth chapter of Matthew where the premise for this book and my previous book - The Agreement were founded, Jesus speaks of a man who had an unpayable debt, the equivalent of $10,000,000. When confronted by his creditor, he demanded the debt to be paid in full on the spot. This man could never have paid the interest, even if he wanted to, but promised to pay the full amount. He cried out begging for mercy, and his creditor forgave his debt on the spot. He forgave his "unpayable" debt!

Later on that same day, the man whose unpayable debt was forgiven approached a man who owed him a small amount of money, equivalent to about twenty dollars. He, too, cried out and begged for mercy. Instead of forgiving the small debt, he demanded that the money be paid on the spot. The man begged and begged for mercy but found none. He and his family were incarcerated.

In the end, this man was turned in by his fellow servants, and the creditor threw him in jail. Sadly, the family he had incarcerated for the debt of a measly twenty dollars was bound in prison and never released because of his unforgiveness.

WISDOM PRINCIPLE: OFFENSE BINDS NOT ONLY THE OFFENDED, BUT THE OFFENDER AS WELL.

You may reason that forgiving someone who has wronged you is optional; however, unless you forgive, you cannot be forgiven.

In this same chapter of Matthew, Jesus explains; whoever will humble himself and become like a little child, [forgiving] is greatest in the Kingdom of Heaven.

WISDOM PRINCIPLE: THE AGREEABLE PERSON IS A HUMBLE PERSON AND THE HUMBLE PERSON IS A POWERFUL PERSON.

It takes a great person, a humble person, an agreeable person to forgive someone when they have been wronged; that is why Jesus is so great. Greater is He that is in you, than he that is in the world.

***

...Kingdom Report...

We're back live with a special top-secret report. The Kingdom continues with its celebration. The music and dancing seemingly never end. The Holy One has a look on His face like someone ready to disclose an extraordinary secret, yet, He is refrained. Could it be another angel of light will be heralded in? More details later...

FIVE

The Day the Music Died

❧

Scene II
The Day the Music Died

All the angels cried, "Holy!" in the direction of the angel of light, and the music flowed. Lucifer beamed with radiant glory as the song of worship surged through him like a mighty ocean under the commands of a powerful hurricane.

Up until Lucifer's debut, the worship of Heaven consisted only of chanting. For ages and ages and ages, the angels had cried, "Holy, holy, holy, Lord, God Almighty; Who was, Who is, and is to come."

Never before had any creature heard such magnificent sounds. Until now, music had only been produced through instruments. But now, they directed their monotonous sounds towards Lucifer, and he transformed them into glorious music.

What a splendid day it had been; the standard of worship had been set. And for many more ages to come, Lucifer led the angelic host in extravagant, grandiose cantatas of worship on the mount.

There were other mountains in the Kingdom, but none compared to the majesty of the Mount of the Congregation, and it became the favored spot in the entire Kingdom.

Each time Gabriel and his third of the angels sounded their trumpets, which sounded at spontaneous times throughout the ages, everyone would gather to hear newer and more innovative sounds of music. The members of the Godhead were always in agreement.

The four living creatures enjoyed the music that was produced on the mount and desired to make sounds like the instrument of worship but could not.

Nevertheless, they were unique in their own way. They represented the masterful abilities of the Creators. They had four faces. One side was the face of something called a man. The angels had never understood what a man was, but they thought it was uniquely beautiful. The other sides had the faces of an ox, an eagle, and a lion. They each had four wings and were able to fly and move any direction at will without turning.

Try as they might, they could not produce the music of Heaven. When they opened their human mouths, monotone sounds were heard. They tried with their lion mouths and startled one another as voracious, loud roars came forth. Their oxen mouths, obviously, could not make any musical sounds; they simply moaned. Their eagle mouths made shrilling shrieks.

Still, they could do nothing but sit on the mount and cry. Age to age, they remained the same. "Holy, holy, holy, Lord, God Almighty; Who was, Who is, and is to come."

The Mount of the Congregation was now known as the Place of His Presence because of the Godhead's desire to dwell where worship had extolled Them. This was where They had been celebrated for many eons now.

The living creatures had not left the site since that first momentous occasion when music had been birthed.

Lucifer was the first created being with the ability to make music.

Until Lucifer was created, music had been restricted to the Godhead alone; only They could produce music. They were accustomed to singing to One another for ages at a time. Oh, there had never been quite so beautiful and grand a music as that. They were the Masters and Creators of the sounds of Heaven.

A different sound was heard in Heaven now.

About a third of the entire host of Heaven had gathered at the Mount of the Congregation. There was an unusual rustling about them. The four living creatures turned their multifarious bodies every which way in a disoriented manner.

Angels beamed here and there while others flapped their wings scurrying to find their places. There was something significantly different about this worship service.

Although no one ever said a thing.

Everyone was always excited to worship. It was an honour offering worship to the angel of light allowing him to play the music of their hearts; since, they could not sing.

Michael and Gabriel had not yet arrived. Their sounds of worship were the cue to usher in the Godhead. They had impeccable timing; when the atmosphere was just the right climate, they signaled for the magnificent entrance of the Supreme-Super Powers.

Two angels near the base of the mountain were making sounds no one had ever heard. Their voices were not filled with praiseworthiness; instead, they released disharmonious, argumentative sounds. They were sounds the Kingdom had never before heard.

Another group of angels began stirring; and they, too, were releasing cacophonous sounds.

Lucifer tried to bring order to the out-of-sorts, abnormal chaos, but the busyness and stirring only heightened.

When out of the north, a thunderous noise was heard. A myriad of angelic beings charging swiftly toward the mount was spotted by one of the angels at the foot of the mount. They flew in perfect congruent order. Row after row; the battalion lines stretched for miles. The leading angel called cadence directing them as they maneuvered in their strategic military formations. With each move he made, as though interconnected, they moved simultaneously with precise synchronicity.

It was as though time had stood still; and in the brevity of that moment, it appeared the Kingdom would be overthrown.

The angels each held an instrument in their hands charging in the direction of the pinnacle of the mount. One of the archangels was leading the horde. It was not clear which archangel could be so brazen as to disrupt the favored time of the Godhead.

It was known that it was not Lucifer because he was at his appointed place. He had always been careful to flow with the order of the Kingdom according to what the Holy One had charted.

No one had ever seen the long, shiny, sharp objects the multitudes of angels were carrying. They flashed them this way and that way! Reflections from the instruments created glares that beamed like laser lights across the mountain. With every wave of the instruments, the peaceful, still air in the Kingdom was disturbed; and with each disturbance, a booming sound was heard. Alternating angels moved their beaming blades diagonally while the others moved theirs the opposite direction. Upon impact, they clinked and clanked creating clashing sounds of infallible praise. It was a rhythmic, percussive performance of perfect synchronicity.

The four living creatures began to roar, moan, cry, and shriek. Darkness covered the skies as the throngs of angels coming from the north eclipsed the radiant light of glory emanating from the chambers of the Godhead.

What was happening to the beautiful Mount of the Congregation?

What was happening in the perfectness of glory?

The clouds rolled in and out with rumblings, crashes, and deafening sounds.

Hordes of angels came from the south side and charged in the direction of the mount with half-moon shaped objects that catapulted a straight stick with a sharp point in the direction aimed.

"Roar!"

"Awk! Awk! Awk!" cried the living creatures.

The Heavens shook as the angels flapped their wings and headed toward the mount in defense of the Kingdom.

Lucifer held his head up high as he stood at the peak of the mount.

No one had ever seen Lucifer's face during a worship concert. His face was always pointed downward in a gesture of humility.

His wings seemed to grow and swell with every note he now intoned. And yet, there were no angels supplying worship for transmutation. His shiny, black tresses fluttered in the wind stirred by the angels' swords clanking overhead.

Clink, clank, clink, clank.

The swords wielded and clashed without interruption, never breaking cadence.

The music had a different sound. Instead of the flowing legato styles, it now shifted and joined the rhythm of the clanking swords. Warfare was intermingled with the fluidity of the divine amorous worship.

Lucifer bellowed, howled, and growled with vociferous sounds of invidiousness.

Where were the Members of the Godhead?

Why had They not been ushered in yet?

The service had begun, and They were not present to receive the mélange of liquid-fire song.

There was no one to receive the worship, and it spilled out in waste. It oozed down Lucifer's chin onto the bottom of his robe and crept slimily down the side of the mount.

Lucifer turned toward the living creatures and the wasted worship foaming from his mouth dribbled and slabbered splashing all over. He foamed at the mouth like a rabid wild dog. The creatures continued to moan, shout, shriek, and roar; their multiple arms and wings waved hither and thither.

With a look of disdain, jealousy, envy, and arrogance; Lucifer swiftly gathered the pungent concoction unto himself and promptly and gluttonously consumed every drop as though someone would try to beat him to it. It had an acrid, bitter taste; and yet, Lucifer savoringly swilled up the matter.

The Godhead remained in Their quarters.

...for Theirs is the honour, the glory, and the power forever and ever, world without end!

***

There was nothing the Godhead did not know. They had been aware of Lucifer's *coup* since the last worship gathering.

The Holy One had noticed something out of order in the

sequence of worship. Nothing could ever elude His great all-knowing wisdom, for she made all things known to Him. Disorder could be easily identified because of the perfect order the Kingdom had been established upon from the beginning of beginnings.

Lucifer had always begun with the transmutation of the four creature's cries.

The music Lucifer produced from the four creatures was a reverential, liturgical canticle. Instead, he had eliminated their portion of worship and produced his own music. He had created his own worship.

The Holy One had perceived an offense in Lucifer earlier on; He graciously waited to give Lucifer an opportunity to rectify the malefaction.

One must remember that the Godhead loved Lucifer, and They delighted Themselves in his worship.

For, what is a king without his subjects?

What is a god without his worshipers?

To say that the most important position for God's subjects is simply prayer and intercession is to say that God is simply a supplier. The Godhead have always delighted in the worship of the Heavenlies.

Nevertheless, Lucifer became offended at the prospect of creating the atmosphere of worship through his music and getting no glory for it. His offense gave birth to arrogance; he exalted himself, and he was filled with pride.

Pride was an attribute belonging only to the Godhead. It was characteristic of Their union alone; no created being had ever dared to indulge in self. Forever and ever, the focus had always been the Godhead.

Lucifer's arrogance ignited a bonfire that burned with conceit, narcissism, envy, strife, and every evil work. It was a perversion of the purity and the virtue of pride.

Pride was not an evil virtue when there was truly someone to be proud of.

Lucifer knew pride as self-indulgence; his pride was dark and stubborn.

The Godhead knew pride as the virtue of boasting in Each Other's greatness.

...for Theirs is the honour, the glory, and the power, forever and ever, world without end!

Crash!

A loud rumble was heard; and for the first time, lightning flashed across the skies. It was a bright, fleeting flash of light that momentarily lit up the darkness in the Kingdom. It was a fiery flare that jaggedly cut through the atmosphere.

The lightning crackled and popped as it tore through the Heavens creating a gaping black hole in the middle of the faultless streets of gold; a porthole opened from the supernatural into another realm.

Lucifer's beauty underwent a radical transformation.

His gloriously full head of hair singed and shrank into his scalp as though it were cringing from his very person. His four wings were ripped off their sockets by an invisible force and fell on opposite sides of the mountain. His body levitated, his back hunched over as his neck stretched into an elongated shape. The jewels that had formed his vesture self-propelled themselves in every direction landing here and there.

His skin turned scaly and calloused. Eyes of blazing fire were replaced by the appearance of dull chunks of coal.

Out of his mouth now gushed forth a burning, hot fire. Not like the fire that had been mingled with the worship, for that fire had been a beautiful cobalt blue with hints of green interspersed, creating a beautiful shade of teal and emerald amidst the intense blue background. The fire of the Godhead was warm and inviting and possessed the powers to incinerate, yet, had never burned before.

Lucifer spewed, hissed, and regurgitated his red, hot fire, intermingled with drab, colorless yellow creating a luster-less orange glow.

Out from behind him appeared an ominous looking snake with no mouth, eyes, or tongue. It curled and twined around his neck choking him, causing the molten fire to flow out of him; it was a part of him. It was a gruesome tail!

The Godhead had never created anything but perfectly formed beautiful works of art.

Lucifer's dragon-like appearance was the result of his inferior attempt at self-creation. No creature was as gruesome and ugly as that of the dragon-like creature he had become.

His angels hissed and sneered as they were hurled one by one down the pit. As they fell they chanted, "Sss. Sss. Sss. Hail, Lucifer, son of the morning. Sss. Sss..."

They continued their chanting until they were in total derision; they turned one on the other. They reached toward Lucifer and cried, "Sssave us! Sssave us!" Their words became muddled and confused, and they cried, "Sss-atan. Sss-atan, save us, Sssaaa-tan!"

Michael led his angels in harmony and order. They wielded their swords cutting down the angels coming from the south.

Michael's angels used their mighty swords that beamed brightly, like lightning contained in a rod, to strike down the opposing angels. Each angel that was smitten was reduced in size and hurled down the deep, bottomless pit, and demons were born.

Gnashing of teeth, moanings, groanings, and guttural sounds were heard as the demons plummeted.

Falling...
Falling...
Falling...
Falling to the edge of doom...
A never-ending pit.
The southern army positioned its troops for attack.
"Ready! Aim! Fire!" cried one of the princes.

Arrows flying; propelled with the speed of light.

They shot at Michael's angels in a futile attempt to subdue them. Nevertheless, not one weapon formed against them reached its target. They aimed, fired but could not make their mark.

Arrows flew above, beneath, and around Michael's angels never reaching their destination. Instead, with missile-like precision, each arrow returned with a deathblow and slew its archer. It was an ambush against their own comrades.

Lucifer had levitated above the thrones while he waged his meaningless, ineffectual battle. His mouth widened and long sharp fangs protruded out of each corner. His tongue projected outward and unfurled with every agonizing sound he made. His arms retreated into his body; his fingers disintegrated exposing sharp claws. It was a total degeneration from the perfectly formed being he had once been.

After this process, he was engulfed by a powerful vacuum that forcibly sucked him under. He was demoted from his elevated position and fell face down on the side of the Mount of the Congregation. His shortened arms and feet clawed feverishly at the terrain fighting to preserve his self-appointed sovereignty as he slithered slowly further down the mount.

The fading angel of light raised his ugly head; his tongue lashed out at the archangel who stood before the dragon with his razor sharp two-edged sword. Michael raised his saber and split Lucifer's tongue in half creating a forked tongue.

Lucifer's ugly tail that hung like a useless appendage revengefully arose and struck Michael hurling him several miles away. In the flash of an instant, Michael was back; he held his sword with both of his muscular arms and wielded a mighty blow. Lucifer was severed in twain; he squirmed and slithered like a beheaded serpent.

The gruesome tail recoiled and uncoiled spasmodically chasing the remaining half of Lucifer's regenerated anatomy. His head peered over the edge of the black hole when suddenly his severed tail assaulted him from behind. Without hesitation, the ugly dismembered appendage vengefully lashed out at Lucifer hurling him down the bottomless pit. The remaining light of Lucifer's glory ignited a bolt of lightning that pierced through the impenetrable darkness of space. His glory was stripped from him by a supernatural spontaneous combustion that snuffed out his light forever.

Darkness, blackness, and obscurity became his spirit, his vesture, and his soul.

His emptiness absorbed the depths of darkness that surrounded him, and they became his glory.

His severed tail wrapped itself tightly around his throat stifling his vicious profanity.

Falling...
Falling...
Lower...
Lower...
Lower...

Leaving behind the glory, majesty, and honour he once wore as his garments of worship.

Lucifer's wings lay listless on the Mount of the Congregation. In an attempt to preserve the integrity and sacredness of the mount, two cherubim retrieved Lucifer's wings and hid their faces with them. They covered the Place of His Presence with the massive wings of worship. Facing each other, they created a canopy, a covering for the place of worship. The ark of a new covenant that could never be breached was formed.

And they cried, "Holy, holy, holy, Lord, God Almighty; Who was, Who is, and is to come! Holy, holy, holy, Lord, God Almighty..." They cried, desperately trying to convince the disappointed Godhead of their allegiance and intent to remain with the Kingdom.

Michael and his angels fought the dragon and prevailed against the hordes of darkness. One third of the entire Heavenly host fell that day.

Only the crying and chanting of angels along with the four living creatures could be heard from the Place of His Presence. The music in Heaven had been subdued. Melancholia blanketed the ranks of Heaven, and the Godhead remained in Their chambers.

***

...for Theirs is the honour, the glory, and the power forever and ever, world without end!

***

The two archangels held their positions on the Mountain of Worship as did all the other angelic beings. No one dared to leave the place unguarded or unprotected. The light of the glory from the chambers of the Godhead was made visible once again. Yet, there was a penetrating stillness and silence that moved like a thick fog over the entire Kingdom.

The four creatures continued their worship without uttering any words. Their spirits now cried to the living God, to the Son of Glory, to the Holy One.

And Heaven was s i l e n t ...

SIX

Exposing the True Works of Darkness

Exposing the True Works of Darkness

I am convinced that the purpose, pursuit, and identity of Satan have been among the most misunderstood secrets of all time.

Remember, a secret is not revealed; it is discovered. Try as I might, I cannot convince you of Satan's true diabolical nature until you discover it for yourself. The people of God must probe what religiosity has clouded for centuries with its theories and self-indulgent hypothesizing.

The presupposition that every thing bad that happens in life is from the devil falsely discredits the power of God.

Where is the power of God when bad things happen to right-standing people? Did Satan win a battle against the God who delights in the prosperity of His children? The obvious answer is a resounding no! Yet, teachings, which attribute the dubious works of the flesh to Satan, have misled many.

I have just completed a conference where many of the greatest speakers of our day delivered powerful messages that had the power to change the thousands who heard them. Yet, a thread of similarity wove its way through each of the speakers' messages that gave credit to Satan's power beyond what God allowed.

I get a disconcerting feeling each time I am in a sanctified, Holy Ghost-filled church, and the leadership mount their pulpits with the idea that a battle over evil must first be waged. My question is always, "Who let the devil in?" They begin their delivery of an anointed message by comparing where we are in our lives at the moment to where we want to go and place the blame on the devil for inhibiting us.

In most charismatic services, a chant of spiritual warfare is led against the attacks of the enemy before God ever gets any recognition or glory. Seemingly, we never get "there" because in the very next service, the comparison is made once again; and Satan is rebuked, demons are bound, and the war continues.

A careful study of the Scriptures reveals that God never called His people to fight His battles. I Chronicles 29:11 states, "Thine, O LORD, is the greatness, and the power, and the glory, and the victory, and the majesty: for all that is in the heaven and in the earth is thine; thine is the kingdom, O LORD, and thou art exalted as head above all."

How much clearer can Scripture get? We have not been called to fight a battle. We are called to love the Lord our God with all our hearts, souls, and bodies.

In the book of Exodus, Moses instructed the children of Israel to stand still and see the salvation of their God.

I heard the Holy Spirit say to me to check my foundation. He instructed me to check my *belief systems*. Check the foundation of my faith. When I say faith, I am not referring to the ability to *faith* something into your life. I am referring to the faith that has been established by the traditions of your parents and their parents. The foundation of faith that has been established by what your pastors have taught you, the foundation of faith of what you basically believe in.

The second thing the Holy Ghost spoke to me was about the confidence I was walking in. What was my confidence based on? Where had this confidence gotten its strength?

I thought it was a confidence based on the truth of the Scriptures.

Quite directly and poignantly, the Holy Spirit said, "Whatever the foundation to your confidence, you did not get it from Me."

The foundation the Church has been operating in is a self-centered confidence. It is an arrogant confidence. A confidence way out of line with God's Word and His plan for the body at large.

The precious Holy Ghost then said that we needed to repent for engaging in a war we were never called to fight.

A greater secret than the secret power of lawlessness, which is why I wrote this book, is the secret of God's original purpose and plan for the Church.

The plan of redemption was not simply to save us from an impending doom to eternal hell. It was never just about saving mankind!

Yes, God loves the whole world that He gave His only begotten Son... But before the Church came along, it was about His purpose. It was about His needs.

Before man needed salvation, God created man for fellowship. God was lonely, so He made Himself a man. Man was lonely, so He made man a woman.

Looming in the background stood a fallen, impotent, powerless archangel with nothing to do.

Have you ever wondered why God did not simply destroy Satan once and for all when He cast him out of Heaven?

Perhaps, God grieved over the loss of one of His angelic sons?

Maybe, God who *is* love could not bring Himself to utterly destroy His own creation.

Perhaps, He had to come up with a plan for a new creature of worship that would replace the fallen archangel before He destroyed him.

Nevertheless, God knew what would transpire in the perfect Garden of Eden long before Satan's dubious plans were carried out.

Before the fall of man, there was no need for a plan of redemption. Everything was perfect in this garden of agreement. Man was in complete agreement with God. The Bible says that God walked with Adam in the cool of the day. This implies a close, intimate relationship between God and man.

When we think of walking with someone, we visualize two people walking side by side, shoulder to shoulder. In the case of Adam and God walking together, the original translation of this passage reveals that they walked nose to nose, facing each other. (I will expound more on this in a later chapter.)

God's plan was all about creating a being, unlike Lucifer, who would choose Him and choose to love Him.

So, we can safely say that God's original *original* plan was all about worship.

My dear friend, Dr. Myles Munroe, was a guest speaker at a conference where I spoke as well. If you know anything about Dr. Munroe, you must know that one of his fortes is Purpose.

He shared a powerful revelation on God's original purpose.

He stated that God's original purpose was for man to subdue the earth and to have dominion. His message was clearly a divine revelation of the importance of God's people living within the Kingdom principles.

In the Kingdom, there are no subjects only sons. We are more than servants in the Kingdom of God.

In religion, we are merely servants. Servants do not have the right to sit in Heavenly places as Christ has promised we would.

The Kingdom of God is the only Kingdom that gives of its wealth and creates a true commonwealth. In God's Kingdom, you enter in with thanksgiving. In earthly kingdoms, you pass through many gates to get to the aristocracy. Jesus taught that the Kingdom of God was already within us.

We cannot operate in the powerful revelation of dominion and Kingdom living until we have first met God's original *original* plan. I am in total agreement with the revelation of Dr. Munroe and stand with him completely. So, allow me to go a step further.

God's original *original* plan was to create a bride strictly for fellowship. Instead, the Church has been engaged in spiritual warfare and before that, steeped in the traditions of men and religiosity. We have torn down strongholds, rebuked spirits, and waged war in the Heavenlies, while the plans of the great Creator have gone unfulfilled.

He is still longing for fellowship.

He is still longing for worship.

John Chapter Four clearly states that the Father is seeking those who will worship Him in spirit and in truth.

I believe in Kingdom living wholeheartedly.

I believe in authority and dominion for the believer. But we cannot achieve these levels until we have moved into that dimension of worship.

Worship is the final dimension of the Spirit. It is the final destination from the outer courts, past the brazen altar, into the Holy of Holies.

When we move past the veil into the Holy of Holies, we enter into a dimension of habitation.

In the Old Testament, the priests could only visit the Holy of Holies once a year, and great sacrifices had to be made to gain access. When Jesus, our Saviour and Lord became the Lamb upon the cross, He paid that debt once and for all. He became the ultimate sacrifice that we might gain entrance to the Holy of Holies.

Once we have gone into that place of habitation that can only be maintained through worship, we move into the realm of the glory of God. Everything you could ever need, want, or desire is in the glory.

It is only when all your needs have been met and surpassed that you can truthfully move into intercession for others. Because when God's presence becomes your joy and your ultimate focus; His joy, pleasure, and focus turns toward you to reward you, to lavish you with the unimaginable.

It is easy to intercede on behalf of others when your needs are automatically met. There are things you do not even know that you want that God is ready to give you. But He reserves these rewards for those who go beyond the veil through worship.

WISDOM PRINCIPLE: THE FRUIT OF TRUE WORSHIP IS JOY.

We must repent for what we have ignorantly done with regards to engaging in spiritual warfare.

It is common knowledge to never engage in a battle you cannot win. And yet, we have struggled, fought, kicked, and screamed at devils completely ignoring the cry of God's heart for fellowship.

We will never win the battle over the devil and his minions until Jesus Christ, Himself, comes and makes them His footstool.

In a previous chapter, I mentioned, "...and there was war in the Heavens..." Are we implying that neither God nor Satan won the battle by engaging in spiritual warfare?

Where are Satan and his minions working? Where can our worship become warfare against the strongholds of the demonic realm? It does not really matter where the battle is raging; whether in the second, third, or fourth heaven - our warfare is invalid there. It is not within our jurisdiction.

Now that we have discovered where the devil does not operate, we must of necessity expose his cover.

You will only find two places in Scripture where Jesus rebukes Satan. Once, when He spoke to Peter and said, "Get thee behind me, Satan."

What did Jesus see in Peter that we have failed to recognize? Matthew 16:22,23 in the Amplified Bible reads, "Then Peter took Him aside to speak to Him privately and began to reprove and charge Him sharply, saying, God forbid, Lord! This must never happen to You! But Jesus turned away from Peter and said to him, Get behind Me, Satan! You are in My way [an offense and a hindrance and a snare to Me]; for you are minding what partakes not of the nature and quality of God, but of men." Jesus rebuked the spirit of offense in Peter.

Perhaps, Peter was focusing on the implications that he might be following a false Messiah. He was afraid of what this scandal might do to his self-important image before the public's eye. If the elders, scribes, and the high priests declared Jesus a liar; it would mean the end of Peter's hopes and dreams of preaching the gospel.

Could it be Peter was offended at Jesus' seemingly weak nature?

Offense has a subtle and cunning way of looking for the most inconspicuous place to carry out its diabolical workings.

The second time Jesus rebuked Satan, He found Himself under the direction of the Holy Spirit being tempted by Satan in the desert. Satan tempted Jesus in an effort to abort His mission, His assignment, and His destiny. "If You are the Son of God, order this stone to turn into a loaf of bread." Of course, Jesus withstood the temptation, combated Satan with the power of the Word, and overcame. This continued for three different attempts, and Satan did not flee until Jesus quoted from the Old Testament, "Thou shalt worship the Lord your God and serve Him only..." Worship was all that was needed to rebuke and dispel Satan's trickery and delusions.

Imagine yourself in a hot desert hungry, tired, and weary. Your ability to reason goes out the window; you must have something solid working on your behalf deep in your subconscious.

Jesus was the Word of God incarnate. He was equipped with exactly what He needed to contest Satan, but the Scripture works only for those who work it.

I know many Christians and non-Christians who know the Scripture but do not have the power to work it!

What is it that makes the Word work for some; and for others, it suppositionally dissipates before they even finish uttering the words out of their mouths?

It is true worship that repels all evil. It is the entrance of God's presence that automatically drives out demonic and satanic activity. The Psalmist wrote, "O magnify the Lord with me and let us exalt His name together!" To magnify means to make larger, to expand.

Satan's strategy is more illusive than we realize. He says to Jesus in the fourth chapter of Luke, "To You I will give all this power and authority and their glory (all their magnificence, excellence, preeminence, dignity, and grace), for it has been turned over to me, and I give it to whomever I will."(AMP)

Perhaps, Satan was taunting Christ with the idea that God had turned over the earth to him and had left Christ out of the inheritance.

"Na-na-na-na-na-na, God gave me control over the earth, and I can do with it what I want, and He gave you nothing but a cross to die on."

He was inviting Christ to move into jealousy, envy, and strife resulting in offense with God. Instead, Jesus rejected the idea of coming out of agreement with the Father and authoritatively puts Satan in his place.

A third time, Satan tries to divert Jesus' attention from His assignment; Jesus simply quotes another Scripture.

Only in one out of the three areas of temptation did Jesus rebuke Satan when offense was present.

Satan's offense was in the area of worship; and consequently, he craves it with everything in him. He was willing to turn over his entire domain of the earth if Jesus would just bow down and worship. He was willing to relinquish everything he had for just one simple gesture of worship.

Satan was unaware of the impending destruction he faced through Christ's death at Calvary. Jesus quoted from the Old Testament and retorted, "Thou shalt worship the Lord your God and serve Him only." Jesus' straightforward response sent Satan into a tailspin, and he fled for a season.

Still, on any given Sunday or at the gathering of any believers' event, you will hear people rebuking Satan.

God has equipped His people with the weapon of the sword of the Spirit - the Word of God. Jesus spoke the Word with authority, ability, weight, and power. He did not engage in spiritual warfare; He simply spoke His Word, and demons obeyed.

The question, then, is when to rebuke and when not to.

The strategy of warfare for the believer is not rebuking demons and Satan but, rather, living a holy and righteous life.

Our warfare is not instituted by helping God win a fight in the Heavenlies. That fight has been waged and won!

In the book of Jude, we find the following description of how angelic beings handle Satan. (Jude 3 AMP) "Beloved, my whole concern was to write to you in regard to our common salvation. [But] I found it necessary and was impelled to write you and urgently appeal to and exhort [you] to contend for the faith which was once for all handed down to the saints [the faith which is that sum of Christian belief which was delivered verbally to the holy people of God]."

This verse deals with the foundation of the believer. The writer of Jude compels us to contend for the faith as it was *originally* given through the words of the Lord, Jesus Christ. How often have you heard teachings from the pulpits in the Church that have, perhaps, disturbed your spirit; but because you heard others teaching the same thing, you believe it? He says, "the faith which is that sum of Christian belief..." This is clearly referring to the foundational belief systems. I am convinced we have entered a realm we were never given permission to enter.

Verses four through six, "For certain men have crept in stealthily [gaining entrance secretly by a side door]. Their doom was predicted long ago, ungodly (impious, profane) persons who pervert the grace (the spiritual blessing and favor) of our God into lawlessness and wantonness and immorality, and disown and deny our sole Master and Lord, Jesus Christ (the Messiah, the Anointed One).

Now I want to remind you, though you were fully informed once for all, that though the Lord [at one time] delivered a people out of the land of Egypt, He subsequently destroyed those [of them] who did not believe [who refused to adhere to, trust in, and rely upon Him]."

And angels who did not keep (care for, guard, and hold to) their own first place of power but abandoned their proper dwelling place - these *He has reserved in custody in eternal chains (bonds) under the thick gloom of utter darkness until the judgment and doom of the great day. (Bold italics added)*

This refers to the principalities that are in the

Heavenlies. It is clear that this battle is fixed because there is no way a demon in eternal chains and under a thick gloom of utter darkness could ever stand up to the forces of God. They are held under this bondage until the judgment and doom of the great day. It does not sound like much of a war.

Verse 8, "Nevertheless in like manner, these dreamers also corrupt the body, scorn and reject authority and government, and revile and libel and scoff at [heavenly] glories (the glorious ones).

But when [even] the archangel Michael, contending with the devil, judicially argued (disputed) about the body of Moses, he dared not [presume to] bring abusive condemnation against him, but [simply] said, The Lord rebuke you!

But these men revile (scoff and sneer at) anything they do not happen to be acquainted with and do not understand: and whatever they do understand physically [that which they know by mere instinct], like irrational beasts - by these they corrupt themselves and are destroyed (perish)."

The archangel, Michael, did not dare revile or speak harshly to the devil. Not because he was fearful of him, but because it would be a personal affront to the Almighty who created him for Michael to engage in a combatant confrontation with Satan.

It is the presence of Jesus in you that rebukes the devil or any of his demons. You were not called to engage in spiritual combat with the satanic. Any involvement with demons is occult activity.

When Jesus and His disciples were in a boat crossing the Red Sea into Gadara, they came upon a raging storm. The disciples became fearful for their lives while Jesus slept in the lower part of the boat. When Jesus awakened, He merely went out and shushed the storm. He did not rebuke Satan or any devil; He rebuked the winds and the rain. His disciples became cognizant of His power over nature. "But the men marveled saying, What manner of man is this, that even the winds and the sea obey Him!" (Matthew 8:27)

As long as Jesus is in your boat, you do not have to rebuke or engage in any warfare. He becomes the Standard of Peace where every element of the natural realm and the realm of principalities must bow down to His presence.

When Jesus and His disciples arrived on the other side of the sea, a demon-possessed man greeted them. The demoniac from Gadara was known as a man with rage and an uncontrollable temper. He ran around naked with no visible signs of self-control.

Offense knows no shame; and much like this demoniac, it will cause you to cast off all restraints. You eventually become lawless.

The demoniac slept in cemeteries among the dead.

Offense relates to things that are dead and clings to incidents of the past refusing to let go.

The longer people stay in the grave of offense, the more the stench of death becomes like a fragrance to them.

The problem with the demoniac was not that he was running around naked or had a problem with self-mutilation; it was an internal problem. This man had suffered an offense that caused him to lose his family, his job, his career, and his own self-respect.

Rather than fearing the devil or the attack of a scared little demon, Christians should fear the ultimate torture in life - being turned over to self.

Romans 1:28-32 describes the horror of being turned over to one's own mind. **Better to have a physical affliction all the days of our lives than to be turned over to self!**

When Jesus approached the man with the demons, he began to cry out, "Why do you torment us?" Christ's presence alone was enough to cause the demons to tremble. They begged Christ to allow them to enter a heard of pigs that were nearby. There was no toiling or warfare involved in this major exorcism.

If Christ be in you and in us all, where then, is the need to fight against demons and devils? All that is needed is to be filled with the presence of God. Greater is He that is in you, than he that is in the world! Satan is no match to the greatness of our God. Matthew 6:13 says, "Lead us not into temptation but deliver us from evil." The best defense against the wiles of the devil is to pray that we will not fall into temptation. Without temptation there is no sin - without sin Satan has no entry into our lives.

You may be asking the question, "What about the Scripture in Ephesians, 'we wrestle not against flesh and blood...'?" Our fight, our struggle is not in the area of flesh and blood, rather, in the spirit realm. This Scripture does not imply you are to literally wrestle with demons in high places; it clarifies the need for agreement among believers. It means the battle is in the Heavenlies, and neither you nor I contribute to the victory of that battle by fighting. "[God] disarmed the principalities and powers that were ranged against us and made a bold display and public example of them, in triumphing over them in him and in it [the cross]." (Colossians 2:15 AMP)

A couple of years ago, Holy Spirit spoke to me about a spiritual paradigm shift. He said the structure of the Church, as it is known today, would begin to change. He gave me a visual of the Church in old Biblical garb as in the days when Jesus walked on the earth. He then showed me a 21st century man in silver lamé type clothing, quite futuristic. It was the 21st century Church!

The difference between where the Church came from and where it is going is as vast as the differences between the cultures of the East and West.

There must be an adjustment in the mentality of believers concerning spiritual warfare. Warfare is not crying, screaming, and conversing with devils. When believers accept a paradigm shift in the theology of spiritual warfare, the Church will then understand its assignment.

The Church has spent so much time trying to refashion and redesign the world by preaching salvation from hell, when in reality the purpose of the Church is much higher.

Christ died for the sins of the world so that He would have a counterpart.

A lover...

A bride...

Someone to worship Him.

No matter how hard we try to change the wicked condition of our world, we cannot. It is the function, purpose, and authority of the Holy Spirit to transform lives through the power of the Scriptures.

Religion imposes rules and guidelines that become stifling, yet, are indigenous of our nature and character not the character of Christ.

Our focus has been aimed at trying to save and rescue others while we continue in our dysfunctional relationships with God.

You are probably feeling a little incensed at my preponderant statement of the Church being dysfunctional. However, the idea of a bride spending all her time warring against a defeated foe is somewhat disturbing.

Has it ever dawned on anyone that Satan is not omnipresent?

I know a woman who gets out of bed every morning, stomps her feet, and recites her daily warfare chant. "Take that, devil, I'm up again. You didn't get me." It is as if her arising is a disappointment to Satan. When, perhaps, Satan does not even know she exists. Again, I assert, Satan is not at all places at all times! The war is in the Heavenlies in the principalities and high places. Your bedroom is not a principality or high place. It is where you find rest and solace from the reality of life.

Satan is not sitting at the foot of your bed every morning waiting to get you. He cannot be at all places at all times!

Look what the Prophet Isaiah wrote to describe Satan: "How you have fallen from Heaven, oh morning star, son of the dawn..." He was one of God's greatest creations. "You have been cast down to the earth, you who once laid low the nations! You said in your heart, "I will ascend to Heaven; I will raise my throne above the stars of God; I will sit enthroned on the mount of assembly, on the utmost heights of the sacred mountain. I will ascend above the tops of the clouds; I will make myself like the Most High. But you are brought down to the grave, to the depths of the pit. Those who see you stare at you, they ponder your fate..."

"Is this the man who shook the earth and made Kingdoms tremble?" (Isaiah 14:12b-16a NIV) This is the one, this little wimp? Look at him now.

When Satan wants to tempt you or distract you, he will use the realm of the flesh and send a Delilah or a Judas to win your confidence, and then, betray you.

After Jesus died on Calvary, He defeated Satan, gave man dominion over the earth and power over all the power of the devil.

The issue is no longer between good and evil, darkness and light, holy and unholy. Spiritual warfare does not involve toiling over demons and addressing them. Instead, it calls for total agreement with the Word of God. Total obedience! Your obedience to the Word is your best defense against evil.

Quit trying to remove the wrong from your life; instead, work on getting the right into your life.

WISDOM PRINCIPLE: THE ENTRY OF TRUTH WILL ALWAYS CAUSE DECEPTION AND ERROR TO BE REVEALED.

Paul admonishes the Church of Ephesus to put on the whole armor of God, to wield the sword of the Spirit, which is the Word of God, and to pray interceding on behalf of the saints. He alludes nothing toward rebuking devils and casting out spirits.

In verse one of Ephesians Chapter Six, Paul exhorts the children to be obedient to their parents. Obedience is a condition of the heart.

In verse four, he encourages fathers to rear their children in the fear and admonition of the Lord. Fear and admonition are conditions of the heart.

In verse five, he speaks to servants to be obedient to their masters, have respect, and be eager to please them in singleness of motive and with all your heart. Again, obedience, respect, and motives are matters of the heart.

In verse nine, he speaks to the masters, and again, gives reference to behaviors of the heart.

WISDOM PRINCIPLE: UNLESS YOUR HEART IS TRANSFORMED, YOUR LIFE WILL NEVER BE THOROUGHLY REFORMED.

And finally, in verse ten and eleven (AMP), he says, "In conclusion, be strong in the Lord [be empowered through your union with Him]; draw your strength from Him [that strength which His boundless might provides]. Put on God's whole armor [the armor of a heavy-armed soldier which God supplies], that you may be able successfully to stand up against [all] the strategies and the deceits of the devil."

Notice, he says **"the deceits"** of the devil. Satan is a master deceiver. The devil will use deception for destruction.

The greatest men who have fallen have fallen because they were deceived. They believed a lie.

"Forasmuch then as the children are partakers of flesh and blood, he also himself likewise took part of the same; that through death he might destroy him that had the power of death, that is, the devil; and deliver them who through fear of death were all their lifetime subject to bondage. For verily he took not on him the nature of angels; but he took on him the seed of Abraham." (Hebrews 2:14) How much clearer can it get? Through Jesus' death, He destroyed the power of death, that is, the devil!

The war was waged and won in the Heavenlies!

It is finished!

It was won when Jesus defeated Satan!

And there was war in Heaven.

Michael and his angels fought against the dragon, and the dragon and his angels fought back, but he was not strong enough, and they lost their place in Heaven. The great dragon was hurled down.

Jesus said, "I beheld Satan coming down like a bolt of lightening." The ancient serpent, called the devil who leads the whole world astray, was hurled to the earth along with his angels.

Does that sound as if you have to keep fighting? **There was war in Heaven; the devil was not strong enough, and he lost!**

"For our struggle is not against flesh and blood, but against the rulers, against the authorities, against the powers of this dark world and against the spiritual forces of evil in heavenly realms." (Ephesians 6:12 NIV) Paul goes on to say, therefore, our battle is not in the flesh. So, in light of that understanding, put on the whole armor of God. He describes the *spiritual* attributes of the armor of God.

The following is a detailed list of the spiritual areas we are to be guarding with our armor.

Your *feet* shod with the preparation of the gospel of peace. Where have your feet taken you lately? Have you spread discord or have you sown peace? The Bible refers to "feet that are quick in running to evil". This is not referring to the size of your physical shoes; it is about your walk with the Lord.

The *breastplate* of righteous living... What have you allowed to seep into your subconscious mind (your heart)?

The *shield* of faith... How many times have you questioned God's plan for your life this week? Are you trusting Him?

The *sword* of the spirit... When was the last time you meditated on the Word of God? Whatsoever things are lovely, pure, just, of a good report, think on these things.

Your *loins* gird about with truth... When was the last time you twisted the truth or blatantly lied? These are all conditions of one's heart. The struggle is not in the sins of the flesh, rather, in the sins of the heart.

The areas Paul referred to do not relate to a person's physical walk; instead, it is related to the condition of one's heart.

The struggle lies within the lack of integrity of the Body of Christ. It is in the arena of the secret, hidden sins. No one can see the hate and envy you may have for someone in your past or your present.

The application of the whole armor of God provides protection from the sins of the heart.

Putting on the whole armor of God will not keep you from fornicating, but it will keep you from lying. It will not keep you from stealing, but it will keep you from spreading gossip.

What really took place during the war in the Heavenlies?

There was anarchy.

There was rebellion against authority.

Mutiny.

The struggle was not in the flesh.

Sexual problems are in reality a problem with rebellion against authority. Even Paul spoke to the members of his own body and brought them into subjection.

The real warfare is to be found within self.

Many are at war within themselves because they have not submitted to the authority of their own convictions. When someone gives in to the works of their flesh, these works have nothing to do with Satan.

The works of the flesh have everything to do with people's inability to submit to authority, even within their own mind to say, "I shouldn't be going to bed with this man because he's not my husband. He does not belong to me. His wife is at home praying for him, and I should not be doing this." Nevertheless, *they rebel against their own conscience.*

If a person cannot listen to their own voice of reason, they will certainly have difficulty submitting to the authority of the man of God.

Do not underestimate the persuasive power of the flesh. Your flesh is not saved. You may say, "I am saved through and through." Your spirit is saved, but your flesh is not.

There are two things that did not get saved when you came to Christ - your conscious mind and your flesh.

Your mind must be renewed by the washing of the water of the Word.

Your flesh must be subdued by the Spirit of God.

Keep in mind that Lucifer and his followers were already established and solidly positioned in Heaven. They had been written into the original manuscript. Salvation was written into their scripts from the beginning of time; and yet, they were deceived.

Do not be secure thinking you cannot be deceived. These truths rival man's theories of salvation. According to the book of Revelation, salvation is a process; it comes to those who endure to the end. "But he that shall endure unto the end, the same shall be saved." (Matthew 24:13)

There are many who claim they honour God's principles with their lips; but in their hearts, they do not even know Him? The Scripture reads, "He answered and said unto them, Well hath Esaias prophesied of you hypocrites, as it is written, This people honoureth me with their lips, but their heart is far from me." (Mark 7:6)

Do not miss what the secret power of lawlessness is doing. Lucifer swept one-third of God's angels away into rebellion. Please note that they did not get caught fornicating. I imagine they were still singing "Holy, holy, holy..." with their mouths, but on the inside they were saying, "Yes, Lucifer, you can do better than God."

There is no way of knowing a person's heart or their innermost thoughts. The Bible says, "The heart is deceitful above all things, and desperately wicked: who can know it?" (Jeremiah 17:9) You can never fully know anyone, not really know every last corner of someone's heart and mind. No one is perfect. Even those sitting in church all their lives with saintly habits and selflessness could be monsters in waiting. They may be filled with unspeakable desires, which may never be acted upon; yet, the right combination could bring the monster to life.

Every person has within a disorienting darkness awaiting its awakening. Without the power of the Word to renew their minds and hearts, this darkness could come to life.

What are you hiding deep within your soul? The secret, the heart of offense could become the combination to your monster. Will you subdue it by making it right with those whom you are offended and by the washing of the water of the Word?

Offense enters with its diminutive form but soon rears its ugly monstrous head and takes over your life. It will unlock the monster within if you choose to wallow in your own emesis of offense.

Offense burns like a fire that ravages everything in its path. The offended one has difficulty hearing and receiving instruction because of the roar of the flames. It burns with an ardent, destructive force; hell pales in comparison to its fury.

We have all probably heard the saying, "Hell knows no fury like a woman scorned."

A lady in Colorado has been featured in the leading newspapers and news casts all over the nation. She has been charged with damaging federal property, injuring a firefighter, and using fire to commit a felony. She is a disgruntled woman, dealing with an offense against her husband. She allegedly started the massive forest fire by burning a letter from her estranged husband. This woman maliciously ignited a fire that has ravaged over 135,000 acres of forest, destroyed 25 homes, and forced the evacuation of 7,500 people. Her offense incited a fire within that burned with the hot coals of envy and unforgiveness.

Getting back to the secret, there was a war in the Heavenlies... Angels were caught rebelling against the organized system of God. And for the first time, there was a division between darkness and light.

Sin is simply a manifestation of an internal problem. We keep trying to cast out the manifestations, but we do not want to deal with the ruling spirit behind the wrong choices. The ruling spirit dominating the Church of Jesus Christ is the same spirit that showed up in Heaven.

This same spirit shows up in a marriage where a wife refuses to submit to her husband resulting in divorce.

This same spirit shows up in a protégé who refuses to submit to his mentor.

It is the same spirit that shows up between two good friends whom God has brought together and their friendship becomes ravaged by the looming effects of dissension and division.

It showed up at the table when Jesus was washing the disciples' feet, and Peter wanted Jesus to wash his entire body.

It showed up at Lazarus' house when his sister, Mary, washed Jesus' feet with expensive ointment. The Bible says that the disciples became offended when she poured out her expensive ointment. Judas became indignant because he was the treasurer and had been stealing money from Jesus' ministry all along.

Judas did not betray Christ for thirty pieces of silver; he betrayed Him because he was offended. The book of John says he entered into a seditious agreement with the Sanhedrin and betrayed Him.

WISDOM PRINCIPLE: OFFENSE BREEDS DISLOYALTY.

This secret sin will show up at Bible study.

It will show up at early morning prayer.

It shows up at church because it is most comfortable in an atmosphere of worship.

*"What is the secret? Perchance, you have already discovered it. The secret is called **offense. IT IS THE SECRET POWER OF LAWLESSNESS.**"* It hides and masquerades behind other non-visible reprobacies such as, bitterness, unforgiveness, strife, and many other non-visible sins.

The Bible instructs us to hide God's Word in our hearts that we might not sin against God. There is a difference between sinning against our own flesh and sinning against God. The sins of the flesh are against the flesh and yield negative results in the flesh. The sins against God are the violation of spiritual law, resulting in loss of His presence.

As long as the Church remains ignorant of Satan's devices, he will be able to take advantage of the ignorant. Hosea said it quite poignantly, "My people perish for a lack of knowledge..." It is not what people do, which destroys them; it is what they do not know or fail to recognize.

You may think Satan is at work in the area of drugs, alcohol, spousal abuse, child abuse, and other addictive behaviors. The big surprise is Satan has no experience in adulterous affairs. His expertise is not in earthly passions and flesh sins.

He has no experience in divorce.

He has no experience in fornication.

He was the worship leader of Heaven. His experience is in worship.

He is remorseful of the secret plot he attempted to carry out in Heaven. That is why he roams back and forth like a lion, as the Bible depicts him, seeking whom he may devour. Satan's vigor and focus is to wear out the saints and sift them as wheat, as Jesus stated in the gospels.

Have you ever lost something that meant the world to you? Something that was rightfully yours; and then, it was taken away. You do not stop yearning for it. You never get over the loss of something you love. You wish somehow it could be restored to you. You keep seeking its restoration.

Satan's mental torment must be incomprehensible.

Imagine the tormenting thoughts having already been positioned in glory; and then, being cast out forever.

The devil is most comfortable in the midst of worship. He enthrones himself in the worship of a person with offense in their heart. Scripture supports this angel was designed to adorn the throne of God. The atmosphere he craves is the one he lost in Heaven.

Perhaps, you are asking, "What about all the sin, degradation, and the vile condition of society?" Religion has taught that evil is most evident in the midst of the heathen and their evil ways.

This dark angel is not as familiar with fornication as many suppose. Satan is more familiar with the atmosphere of a worship service than he is with a topless bar.

The devil was and is a worshiper. He has one of the greatest worship followings through the industry of secular music. The phenomenon of rock-n-roll and the ever-popular pop-culture did not evolve from Elvis' hips; it is a strategic work of darkness.

As I mentioned earlier in a previous chapter, music in and of itself is not evil; it is the content or the impurity of the vessel that corrupts the music.

Lucifer lost his position in Heaven; and now, his mission is to keep the Church from filling that position.

The devil is not involved in the areas of immorality as he has led the Church to believe. Remember, Satan is a spirit and works in the realm of the supernatural. Sexual immorality, alcoholism, and such are all sins of the flesh committed by human beings in the natural realm.

Sins of the flesh will ultimately lead to the destruction of a man's soul if not dealt with but are not the cause of the soul's destruction.

You may try to pin everything evil on the devil; however, the real problem lies in the power of your choice.

SEVEN

Choices, Choices, Choices

Choices, Choices, Choices

How often have you heard someone detailing his or her weekend escapades and blaming the devil? "I have a weakness with pretty women" or "good looking men". "I was out Friday night, and before I knew it, I found myself sleeping with this guy..." "The devil tricked me, and I fell for his cunning ways."

Your flesh led you.

Your predicament was a result of your choices.

Satan was nowhere in sight, Your choice of people, places, and circumstances facilitate your desire to sin.

You can hear more praise given to the devil during a time of testimonials than you hear God's name mentioned.

"The devil did this; the devil did that; the devil destroyed my marriage." The devil, the devil, the devil.

No! You made a choice.

You do not have a marriage problem.

You have a rebellion problem. Somebody in that relationship is in rebellion.

Kids do not have drug problems. They do not just wake up one day and have a desire for drugs. It is a problem with rebellion.

**

The book of James depicts sin as a gradual succession of choices.

WISDOM PRINCIPLE: LIFE IS A SEQUENCE OF CHOICES; THE QUALITY OF YOUR LIFE IS CONTINGENT UPON THE CONSISTENCY OF RIGHT CHOICES.

Life is a sequence of choices.

You can make one right choice; but if you stop making right choices, the quality of your life flows accordingly.

Where is Satan's involvement in this case? It has nothing to do with the devil.

Jesus said, "Behold, I give you power over *all* the power of the devil."

Satan does not know anything about most of the things we classify as sin. Having a one-night fling has nothing to do with the devil; it has everything to do with choices.

If a person has one too many drinks, the only way to be delivered from that bondage is to make the right choice. He has to decide, "This is going to be my last drink." There is no devil making him drink; it is a choice.

The beauty of choices is every time you make a right choice all of Heaven backs you up. You have the power of the glory of God at your disposal when you choose righteousness.

The devil does not have to be present for someone to fornicate. Fornication is not a spiritual problem; it has to do with the flesh. It is not a demonic activity.

Remember, Satan's arena of operation is to stop true worship from entering Heaven.

So, would the real devil please stand up? Please do not become offended by the implication of being called a devil. Jesus pulled no punches in His response to Peter in Matthew 16:23 when He said, "Get thee behind me Satan."

The sooner we accept fault, the quicker we become what God intended for us to be.

I think we have met the real enemy in our lives, and he is called *self.*

My father was an alcoholic; does that mean I follow in his footsteps?

I make the choice.

It is no different than you being upset at homosexuals marching for gay rights. They are simply trying to find a scapegoat for their choice of lifestyle.

Still, it is a choice!

Strong sexual desires are natural in most men, however, that does not mean they are granted the right to sleep around any time they have a sexual craving.

It is a matter of choice.

Everything is a matter of choice.

My good friend and member of my church, Dr. Zonnya, has written a tremendous book entitled: *Stop Setting Goals and Start Choosing Results!* She teaches on the power of making choices that equal results instead of setting goals. Our minds cannot process the idea of setting goals because it is predisposed to making choices and getting results.

We have removed the disgrace of sin making iniquitous living inconsequential.

I was counseling someone about a child that was going through a rebellious stage in life and had made some wrong choices.

My counsel to the parent was to make the child feel shame for what he had done. The response was typical of most overindulging parents. "God does not want us to feel shame."

Naturally, our forgiving and loving Father does not bring shame upon His own; instead, the child brought shame upon himself by the choices he made. The child must feel embarrassed for the wrong choices made.

Your choices will either yield positive results or negative results. The choice is up to you!

A preacher can instruct his people to abstain from sexual immorality, to avoid smoking, drinking, and swearing until he is blue in the face.

For years, I tried keeping people out of sin by admonishing them on what they should not do; and still, there was no change in their behavior. I finally gave up; reasoning, these people do not want to change the way they live.

Everyone must have their own epiphany for change. You must have your own moment of sudden intuitive understanding where change becomes essential to your spiritual growth.

WISDOM PRINCIPLE: CHANGE IS THE ONLY CATALYST TO THE CHARACTER OF CHRIST.

God is concerned about what occupies a man's heart and not his flesh-driven desires. The book of Proverbs says, "As a man thinketh in his heart so is he." The temptations of the flesh, in time, will come into subjection to the power of the Holy Ghost.

Prayer does not change a person's will to sin; sin is a choice. When you come fully into submission to authority with honour in your heart, you will be able to live in your flesh as a righteous person.

King David was a man with many shortcomings. His continual self-searching for wrong motives, wrong thoughts, and his passionate pursuit of God made him great. In Psalm 139:23, he passionately cries out to God, "Search me, O God, and know my heart: try me, and know my thoughts: And see if there be any wicked way in me, and lead me in the way ever-lasting."

Believers are quick to judge and act against abortion, homosexuality, and pornography. The real issue behind these obvious sins is much deeper. The problem begins in the heart.

Abortion is more than just the killing of babies; it is the eradication of tomorrow's great leaders.

Too many believers have taken the position of placing much of the blame on a fallen, powerless angel.

Yet, there was no fornication in Heaven.

There was no alcohol in Heaven.

The Bible does not credit these works to the devil. These are works of the flesh.

You cannot cast out a devil of alcoholism when it is a flesh problem.

A man suffering with lust is simply making a choice to yield to ungodly thoughts.

The Scriptures tell us we are to cast down every vain imagination and bring every thought to the obedience of Christ.

Every man, every woman, every child of God deals with impure thoughts and must choose to bring them under subjection to the obedience of Christ.

The root of many of the wiles Christians deal with is found in their fearlessness and rebellion to spiritual authority. Evil thoughts find their essence and subsistence through hidden rebellion.

Rebellion against God's Word...

Rebellion against spiritual and natural authority...

Rebellion against the convictions and promptings of the Holy Spirit.

Every thought comes to fruition when mixed with the witchcraft of rebellion. Remember, the sin of rebellion is as witchcraft. It is like a big caldron where thoughts seethe, stew, and boil over and cast their spell upon their victims.

Lucifer did not recognize the power of authority and spiritual protocol of Heaven; and, consequently, was renamed Satan and was banished from glory.

The problem, thus, is not rampant sexuality or alcoholism. The problem is rebellion; the *sine qua non* of a sin driven society.

The root of the problem lies in the choices of those who resist authority and the instruction of a man or woman of God.

Much of my tenure in ministry, I have labored in trying to make people believe the devil does not have as much power as he is accredited. Perhaps, this does not sit well with your theology; however, my foundation is the truth of God's Word.

Christians struggle because they refuse to acknowledge their own weaknesses choosing, instead, to hide behind the myth of an overpowering devil.

The Church has provided sanctuary for people who do not want to turn from their sin. In the Byzantine era, people could claim sanctuary by running into the church, whether they were guilty or not, and the priests would allow them to stay in return for special favors.

It is distasteful to think that a man of God could be easily bribed. However, it is not much different when you choose to place the blame of your faults on the devil and then hide under a false pretense of spirituality as you sit unrepentant in your church.

I am of the belief that every existing thing has a counterpart, and nothing is inert. Everything has some form of effect on each of our lives.

Unquestionably, there is good and evil in this world. There is darkness and there is light. However, I have never been content with the excuse the Church has adopted for the blame of its wrongdoings: called the devil.

The devil has become the scapegoat! Perhaps, the one-liner, "The devil made me do it!" fell into the wrong hands and became a doctrinal excuse for sinning. Please do not misunderstand what I am saying; I believe the devil exists, but I do not believe he is as devilish as we make him out to be. It is true; he desires to destroy what God builds, except, that he does not have the power; unless, it is given to him.

Satan's **strategies** are aimed at establishments of worship for the purpose of carrying out his mission.

His **mission** is not to destroy the average Christian; rather, to abort the Father's quest to recruit worshipers.

His **objective** is to disqualify you from meeting the qualifications of a worshiper through the strategy of offense.

Satan was created for worship; how "devilish" can that be? Perhaps, this monster called the devil is a totally different being created by the Church to cover up its indiscretions.

A missionary from Africa was quoted saying, *"You want to see real devil? Get up in the morning and look in mirror, you will see real devil."*

If the devil were the source of all our problems, the solution would be to line up everyone dealing with lust, fornication, adultery, and any other perverseness; summon an anointed man of God, and cast out every devil.

If it is a "devilish" thing; then, the anointing of the Almighty God who cast Satan out of Heaven in the first place should be enough to undo his works. How can a little demon working in a Christian's life come under the power of the Holy Spirit in an anointed service and not be instantaneously exorcised?

You will instantly know when someone dealing with a real devil comes into your church. If there is any kind of anointing flowing, that devil will begin to go crazy from torment.

The devils Jesus dealt with recognized His anointing and were tormented at His very presence.

Do you have enough of Jesus' character in you to torment devils if they come around you?

Again, I assert, it is not a demonic problem. It is a flesh problem. If God were to begin to administer deliverance in our churches, there would probably be nothing left but a valley of bones in sanctuaries all over the world. Flesh burns easily under the anointing!

It is not until a person comes into submission to the voice of authority that true freedom is enjoyed. There are things in your life that will not change except you submit yourself to spiritual authority.

The problem with people falling into flesh sins is directly related to the fact that most people are simply abstaining from things their appetites still desire.

Sin becomes reprehensible when you allow the Spirit of the Lord to write His Words in your heart and mind.

To hate sin and be repulsed by its fruit is proof the Word of God has been engrafted in you.

Everything begins with a thought.

Allow God to write His Word in your mind and your thoughts will change. Your thoughts will govern the results in your life because you will begin to make right choices.

WISDOM PRINCIPLE: THOUGHTS GOVERN CHOICES.

The office of a shepherd is not to simply watch over the sheep, but to shear them, to protect them from their own foolishness, and occasionally, break their legs in an effort to teach the stray lamb a lesson.

Not too long ago, I preached a message about things that do not always change when you get saved. If you were a liar, a cheat, or had a criminal background; you still have the same things working against you, even, after you are saved. The only difference is, now, you are saved. There is obviously hope for change; however, you may still have the same nasty habits. If you were a liar before you came to Christ, now you are a saved liar.

The Bible says, "Let this mind be in you which was also in Christ Jesus." Regeneration is a process that begins with your thoughts. "As a man thinks in his heart, so is he."

You may query in your mind that old things are passed away; behold, all things have become new as the Scripture states. However, if you read the rest of that passage found in II Corinthians 5:17; it reads, "Therefore if any man be in Christ, he is a new creature: old things are passed away; behold, all things are *become* new." The operative word is **"become"**.

A dog will always be a dog. You cannot teach a dog to speak. You may teach him to sit and roll over, but he is still a dog. In all of God's creation, humans are the only ones He gave the power to become. You can become whatever you desire!

I am convinced the only way a person can change from being who they were before receiving Christ is to submit to spiritual authority.

WISDOM PRINCIPLE: SUBMISSION TO SPIRITUAL AUTHORITY IS THE ONLY PATH TO REFORMATION.

You may pray, you may fast, but you will always deal with your old habits until you submit to your spiritual authority. You must have the help of God through a spiritual leader.

Deliverance comes through submitting your flesh to the discipline of serving others.

People with marital problems have not reached their demise because they have irreconcilable differences. Think about that statement: *Irreconcilable differences.* There is never a situation that becomes irreconcilable; all that is needed is for someone to find the agreeable factor.

It is a problem with structure.

It is a problem with authority.

It is a problem with offense in one of the party's heart.

There is a war.

There is definitely a struggle. Victory does not come until you move into submission to the voice of authority; be it directly from God, His Word, or from a man of God. **Learning to walk in submission to spiritual authority is the only way to change the flesh!**

The world has reached its zenith in rebellion, and the result has been a rude awakening of the need for boundaries. Sadly, the Church saunters along with its religious mindsets of *I'm okay, you're okay.*

Secular schools, youth organizations, and drug abuse programs are now providing stricter, more stringent guidelines for our generation of troubled youth. They have discovered the importance of limitations and boundaries. Studies have proven these young people want and desire these restrictions. In these programs, their privileges are cut off; they are forced to deal with the consequences of their choices, and are required to follow every instruction to the letter.

WISDOM PRINCIPLE: TRUE FREEDOM NECESSITATES BOUNDARIES.

If the Church continues to offer its watered-down sermons requiring no blood-washed living, it will soon lose its voice. Without authority and boundaries, there is no hope for reformation.

Where does the Bible say the war was waged? In Heaven. Anarchy and rebellion were released against the standardized authority in Heaven. Lucifer wanted to change the system by undermining the authority of God.

The abomination in Heaven was not fornication, drinking, or any of man's outward, sordid deeds. The war had nothing to do with the misconduct frequently attributed to sins that separate one from God. The problem was rebellion. Wanting to be "independent", wanting to be "off to one's self", wanting to "do one's own thing"; these phrases are all synonymous with rebellion.

Many Christians want to blame the devil for activities that are nothing more than flesh gone wild. When you get the inside right, the outside will follow.

It is quite disheartening as a pastor to see Christians come into my church thinking they have arrived because they have stopped drinking, using drugs, or are living a celibate life. Yet, they are empty, shallow and have no concept of the requirements for an intimate relationship with the Lord.

You may be wondering why I am so adamant about proving that warfare is not a necessity in the life of the believer.

The more time believers spend in rebuking the devil and fighting demons, the less time they allot to the worship God so desperately desires. If you spend all your energy fighting devils, there is little or no time left for loving on the Lord.

We are lovers not fighters!

Even in a marriage relationship, if the husband spends all of his time working, he will be too tired to become intimate with his spouse in their home-life.

I know this goes against traditional teaching, but it is these types of traditions that make the Word of God ineffective.

Can you see the vicious cycle?

You spend all your time fighting a defeated foe and very little time in God's presence.

The Church is an organism made of spirit and flesh. God has pre-equipped us for victorious living. While no one stays on course all the time, He has equipped His children with the ability to get up and get back on track, even, when one falls.

Flesh will be flesh. The spirit is willing, but the flesh is weak. The spirit man must be filled with the Word of God to overcome the flesh.

This is not a theology about being perfect; it is about agreeing with God's Word. Period! There comes a time in our walk with the Lord when we do what we do because we are in total agreement with God's plan and not simply out of obeying some long list of rules.

Traditionally, the Church's focus has remained on trying to perfect the flesh. Our flesh will eventually burn along with all of its accomplishments and failures. Attention to perfecting the spirit man within should be the focus and not that of the flesh. The Holy Spirit is not looking for perfect people; He is looking for people of precision - one who does precisely what He instructs. How well do you follow instructions? Can He trust you to do exactly what He tells you?

Until the alcoholic develops a different taste, he will continue to drink. We cannot pray him through beyond the power of his own choosing. It is not a matter of casting a demon out of him.

Until those who are still engaging in sexual immorality end up with some incurable disease or some form of STD, they will maintain the same sinful lifestyle.

I heard about a man who lived in Texas and had some fling in California. He said he just "slipped". That was a two-thousand-mile slip. He slipped from responsibility into adultery.

Every work of the flesh has its consequences.

For years, I preached messages of conviction about sin; and, still, it had no lasting impact. My congregants would abstain for a season, only to become ensnared by the same temptations soon after. They had not chosen to walk away from their sins. I changed my philosophy and learned to allow the Holy Spirit to bring people under His conviction.

When the sinner hates and abhors his sin within his own heart, he will then desire to change.

Unless a person chooses to yield to the convictions of the Holy Spirit, the cocaine user will continue to snort until his nose rots through to his brain.

Until the alcoholic drinks to the point where his liver is destroyed, he will not change.

People do not need nor do they want someone telling them what they should or should not do. A person's body will eventually give off the telltale signs of their choices.

The inevitable truth is at some point you must make the choice. You may choose the agreeable route of the Holy Spirit or the difficult route of creating your own fate.

For generations, religion has taught wearing makeup is sin claiming it promotes lust. Yet, a man with a holy appearance may walk into your church this Sunday and burn with lust for women wearing no makeup.

The Church has misunderstood the whole concept about righteous living! The works of the flesh are the least of God's worries for the Church. God is concerned about the condition of men's hearts.

People may attempt to deceive those around them, but they cannot deceive the all-knowing God. You may smile on the outside and pretend your choices have no consequences; but when the final count is in, the flesh will have reaped its consequences.

Consequences: they will become evident in your life at some point or another.

The Bible says the wages of sin is death. Each time you sin, something good that God had already predestined for you to have dies. It is not that God wants to give one person more than He does to another; God wants to bless you, but you must continue to make the choices that keep you on the path.

It is not the sins of the flesh, which hinder the Church; it is the condition of men's hearts.

Life is a sequence of choices.

When a man decides to quit drinking or to quit his involvement with pornography, it will be by his own choosing and not by the laying on of hands. It is his choice to quit!

The sins of the flesh are not what hinder the Church.

The war waged in Heaven was about Lucifer choosing to rebel against the order of the Kingdom. It was never about a Light beer or a pack of cigarettes, nor was it about a Penthouse magazine or a Bathsheba. There was no strong alcohol at the last supper. Yet, there was war at the table.

I can just picture Judas as he sat and watched the love and agreement that flowed between Jesus and His beloved: Peter, James, and John. Imagine the jealousy and envy in Judas' heart, which caused him to become offended. He was the treasurer, and he had invested as much time in Christ's ministry as the others; yet, his relationship with Christ was not on the same level. Judas' struggle was not about sins of the flesh; it was about being offended.

The Church has placed the emphasis of wrong on the

very things the devil has directed attention to - the flesh.

Satan, with his trickery, causes God's people to concentrate on works of the flesh; so they will never work on the pride, the lying, the backbiting, the discord - the very things that God says He truly abhors.

"These six things the Lord hates, indeed, seven are an abomination to Him: A proud look [the spirit that makes one overestimate himself and underestimate others], a lying tongue, and hands that shed innocent blood, A heart that manufactures wicked thoughts and plans, feet that are swift in running to evil, A false witness who breathes out lies [even under oath], and he who sows discord among his brethren." (Proverbs 6:16-19 AMP)

These abominations are transgressions purposed by an evil heart motivated by offense. They are premeditated offenses against God's ordinances. They are a direct violation opposing the nature of God: His Spirit.

According to the sixth chapter of Proverbs, there is no reparation after a sudden calamity comes upon the offender. Like a Humpty Dumpty, they will be broken beyond remedy.

Oh, that these transgressions were as easily dismissed as a nursery rhyme, but their consequences are irrefutable. This is not to imply that the offender is without hope. **Opportunities for a new beginning are available after the offender has made restitution for the offense.** However, the losses can never be regained.

WISDOM PRINCIPLE: OFFENSE IS THE POISON THAT UTTERLY DESTROYS FRUITFUL SEED.

Fields and fields have become barren wastelands where seedlings have succumbed to the poisonous effects of offense and have withered and died. The causticity of offense has a far-ther reaching effect than one realizes. It attacks fruit-bearing seed like a potent herbicide that neutralizes life.

There are countless who sit in their church congrega-tions with haughty eyes thinking, "Who does that pastor think he is, telling me how to live?" Many sit smugly in their pews week after week thinking, "He is not speaking to me because I do not abuse drugs or commit adultery."

Remember, Jesus said, "It is not what a man puts in his mouth that corrupts him; it is what comes out of his mouth." Out of the abundance of the heart the mouth speaks! **Whatever is in your heart will eventually come out.**

The works of the flesh are sins prompted by external factors; they are appetites and impulses of the carnal nature. These sins are not committed as a result of the secret power of lawlessness, which is offense. Instead, these works of the flesh are human nature without God; they are results of walking in the flesh.

Choose to walk in the Spirit.
Choose to walk in forgiveness.
Choose to walk in humility.
Choose life!

***

In the Kingdom of God, life is a sequence of choices. **Choose God and you choose life.** Just as Lucifer elected to become offended, he chose to rebel; he chose to be arrogant - you must also choose which direction your life will take.

Regardless of how good or bad your circumstances may appear at the moment; remember always, things can change in the course of twenty-four hours or for that matter in the twin-kling of an eye.

Will you be ready?

EIGHT

True Worship Is Born

❧

Scene III
True Worship is Born

Everything happened in what seemed like the twinkling of an eye; yet, much time had passed since Lucifer's insurrection.

The great doors of the Godhead's chambers were eternally tall. It gave them the appearance of stretching several Heavens above. They were made of two unblemished pearls that had been fished out from the Crystal Sea near the Place of Crossing. Words were carved into them resembling the shape of cherubim wings. Hinges made of gold filigree supported their massive weight and connected them to the transparent gold walls. These walls did not reveal, nor divulge any private communions between the Godhead; they simply provided an endless appearance to the limitless quarters - for nothing could ever contain or confine the glory of the Godhead!

The Holy One made His way beyond the massive doors, and they closed automatically behind Him with a resounding thud that echoed through the vestibule leading to the great hall. A mist of fragrant incense seeped its way out from under the great doors upon their closing. It billowed into the hallway like a soft snow falling, trailing behind Him.

The prism curtain behind the thrones tinkled and chimed as the fragrant, refreshing air escaped the holy chambers and moved down the arched colonnade.

He sat upon His throne in full splendor and majesty as though nothing had transpired.

Lucifer's angelic massacre was now only a vague memory. His capital crime of treason had been brought to the incorruptible justice of Heaven and he was sentenced to eternal damnation.

The angels looked at the Holy One with a quizzical look, they had no idea what had transpired during those long, grueling ages when the Godhead retreated to Their chambers.

The Holy One announced: "We have devised a plan to restore the music of worship to the Kingdom."

"But where is the Almighty?" many questioned among themselves.

"Where is the Son of Glory?" shouted another.

In the stillness of that moment, out of nowhere, one of Gabriel's angels began shouting,

"Hal—le—lu—jah!"

"Halle—lu—jah!"

"Hallelujah!"

Three times, his lips formed the word he had never heard nor uttered before.

The Holy One pursed His lips and, with a twinkle in His eye, smiled softly in an approving manner.

Everyone stood motionless. Neither of the remaining archangels, nor the entire angelic host, knew what the word meant.

The Holy One stood on the platform of His throne made of ornately carved gold, with massive legs resembling a lion's paws. A white marble slab with perfectly symmetrical gold veins reflected the brightness of the Godhead. Two enormous trees flanked the stage that would later provide a touch of Heaven in the Garden of Eden, as the tree of life and the tree of the knowledge of good and evil.

The Holy One extended His mighty arms over the congregation of angels. His majesty and holiness blanketed the Heavens as far as the eye could see. It came down like soft beads of silver rain that did not saturate their garments. Their exclusive purpose was for sheer pleasure. They rolled off the angels like mercury giving them a sensation like the caressing touch of an angel's feather, then dissipated as they landed softly on the streets of gold increasing their brightness. The angels simultaneously and involuntarily exploded into applause and shouted for joy,

"Hallelujah!"

"Hallelujah!"

"Hallelujah!"

It was the universal language of worship.

The sounds of their antiphonal hallelujahs reverberated throughout.

The curtain of prisms furled and sparkled glistening in response to the adulation. It was a spontaneous act of worship.

As if by an internal knowing the entire host of Heaven simultaneously took in a deep breath, creating a huge vacuum in the atmosphere. They were moved by their inner connection to the Holy One, and they were amazed and astounded.

Clouds scampered here and there and billowed in approval as the angels exhaled.

Unbeknown to them, at that very moment somewhere far below Heaven's surface in a place called earth, man was formed.

And man became a living soul reaching for its Creator.

The Almighty had made a special trip to a galaxy near the heart of the earthly universe, which sat at the epicenter of the Godhead's multi-universes.

He created a perfectly imperfect world for man. The Almighty could produce nothing but perfection, so He left Himself out of that which He had created; thus it was perfectly imperfect.

This was a very special place among the galactic solar bodies. It was a hyper-baric chamber designed specifically for His new creation.

He had fashioned this planet as a geosphere that produced its own life. This globe was filled with a magnificent substance called water. He liked it so much He covered over half of it with the clear, flowing matter. He made it sparkle with a turquoise color that reflected the blue skies above. This liquid was the essence of the Almighty's own inner Spirit. Because it was from within Him, a part of His very being, the waters frantically and desperately struggled with violent ardor laboring to return back to Him. They crashed against the terrain of the new planet.

Waves...

Shhhhh. Shhhhh. Shhhhh. Shhhhh.

The clouds above, likewise, desperately tried to recover the Godly essence and by way of evaporation retrieved portions, but the Almighty forced them to release it.

Once in another time, after man had been in existence

for a spell, the Almighty had allowed the thirsty clouds to retrieve much of the essence because mankind had forgotten about the grand design the Godhead had laid out. Unlike the parched clouds that clamorously thundered for His essence, and had no other purpose but to passionately yearn for the Creator, man had looked to himself for joy and pleasure.

Pit...

Pit... pit... pit...

Pitter...

Pitter-patter...

Pitter-patter...pitter-patter-pitter-patter.

So, He let it rain for a doomful forty days and forty nights. The Almighty's fury had been released through His Spirit that flowed out in the gentle liquid form and had now become nihilistic.

The Heavens became dark weighing heavy with the flowing substance. The clouds tumbled around in turmoil. Some rolled in while others receded but never gave way to each other nor did they allow the sun to shine.

The great nimbus clouds hovered high above encouraging the nimbostratus below as they gushed forth as though the Heavens had retained the oceans until they burst.

From the north blew an arctic wind that clashed with the warmth of the unyielding southern gales creating an avalanche of water. The cloudburst emptied out its fury over the land. Thunder boomed and lightning cracked and the rain fell...

And fell...

And fell.

It was a dark time on the little planet; soon, the Almighty commanded the clouds to move out and restricted them to a cycle. He promised never again to allow the Heavens to inundate the globe for the purpose of annihilation.

He assigned one spectrum of colors from the bow that surrounds His throne to commemorate His promise, still leaving Him with a myriad of colors too wonderful to describe. It appeared like a halo in the sky, and it served as a reminder of the day when His plenipotentiary glory had been poured out by rain.

He constrained the Heavenly corona of colors on the northern and southern brims of the sphere. Their intense vividness of color was too much to store in one location. At night they splashed their colors like fluorescent paint upon a backdrop of intense blackness; and by day, they provided the primary colors which filtered the light of the sun adding color to an otherwise black and white galaxy - for in this galaxy there is only night and day, black and white.

But for His glory, this would be a rather dull place.

These remarkable, inextinguishable lights paraded around with pride and were but a glimpse of the wealth of colors belonging to the Godhead. Purples beyond the depths of a violet, yellows as intense as a field of sunflowers on a sunny day. A blue as vivid as the blue on an exotic peacock feather. Lavish greens like fresh spring grass after a cool rain.

The Almighty set the earth on its axis and sequenced its rotation cycles in conjunction with the celebratory festivals of Heaven. So, it is during these endless seasons the lights sing and dance and can be seen for miles.

To this day the waters continue to splash, spill, and crash against the shores of the land in desperation for His presence. It is said, that in the deepest parts of the oceanic substratum the force of the glory is too omnipotently excellent for man to comprehend and can never be explored. It is in these depths that the glory radiates with such brilliance and splendor, the brightness of it eclipses the sight and it appears as blackness.

One tiny drop of water carries within its molecular composition the power, which makes up the eminent forces of the oceans, seas, and rains because it contains the glory of the Godhead.

The Almighty had spent six days creating, designing, and perfecting every accoutrement of the ecologically sustained sphere to house His finest creation - man.

Unlike Lucifer, this creature would be led by his own conscience and choose by his own volition to worship the Godhead. This would be a creature without the glory and beauty of the Master's faultless touch; it would be molded and fashioned from its own terrain.

Man's beauty and glory would come from his power to choose to be like the Creator. A transformation would take place by the power of knowledge that would require an exchange. Man could replace his terrestrial body with a celestial one for the price of his soul. That price would be the freedom to choose based on man's knowledge or the freedom to choose based on the Almighty's knowledge. The differentiating factor would simply be man's knowledge versus God's knowledge. This would secure him a place among the immortals.

Immortality for mortality.

Celestial for terrestrial.

Heaven for hell.

Back at the Kingdom, the Holy One continued with the solemn assembly. With no hesitation in His thunderous voice, He proclaimed the sagacious plan of the Godhead that caused a reverential fear to come upon the Kingdom and spellbound all who watched.

The living creatures appeared indistinctly as though through a mist listening in on the masterful plan.

Blast of air...

Whoooooooooosh!

"The Almighty has created Earth!" bellowed the Holy One.

The angels sighed, some gasped, while others cooed at the prospect of a new, reformed instrument of worship. The last creature was named Lucifer; this one must be named "Earth"; they thought to themselves.

The Holy One, transparent and pure, giggled softly and said, "No, no. Earth is a place much like Heaven, with the exception, that Lucifer has been given the right to roam throughout the land."

The angels' faces fell, and a look of concern came over them.

Whoooooosssssh!

"The Almighty will one day judge and condemn Lucifer for his treason. But the focus of the Kingdom is, now, to raise up a new instrument of worship." He announced proudly and resolvedly.

"I wonder if this new creature the Holy One speaks of will look like Lucifer?" questioned the angels among themselves.

"Will he filter our worship like Lucifer did?"

"Will he be adorned like the last worship leader?"

Perceiving their thoughts, the Holy One spoke, "Never again will there be an opportunity for a created being to loftily exalt himself above the Godhead. We are now looking for those who will worship in spirit and in truth."

"I'll worship and create the music you desire, Holy One," cried one of Gabriel's messenger angels.

"That can never be," said the Holy One.

Whoooosssh!

Some of the angels snickered and some tittered at the angel's comment.

"Worship and music will never come from Heavenly beings; it must come from those who choose to worship of their

own free will. Someone who will say no to Lucifer's entice-
ments with abandonment of adoration for the Godhead."

"But, Lucifer is no match to the power of the Godhead,"
hollered one of the angels several clouds behind Michael.

A trumpet sounds. Tat ta da da!

"We have given Lucifer or Satan as his followers call
him, the power over the air in this place called Earth."

Gabriel blows his trumpet without being prompted.

Tat ta da da! Tat tat ta ta ta dada!

"He will rule until I defeat him and strip him of his
power," said the Son of Glory looming from behind the curtain
of icicle-like prisms.

The Holy One faced the Son of Glory and without hesitation receded to His throne and agreeably acquiesced.

The angels began questioning:

"What does He mean?"

"How will He defeat Satan; He has never known or
experienced combat?"

"It goes against His character."

"How can this be?"

A pounding drum, timpani boomb...

Boomb   bomb   boomb   boomb!

boomb   boomb   boomb

The Almighty made His grand entrance and sat on His
emerald throne. The four living creatures flew back a few yards
in honour and reverence.

"I have created man..." thundered the Almighty.

"Man," the angels thought to themselves, "a being like
the beautiful face on the living creatures?"

The Almighty continued, "The man looks like Us and
has the capacity to house the presence of the Holy One by his
own choosing, but it will take the sacrificial death of the Son of
Glory to make man worthy."

Trumpet fanfare...

Tat ta da da!

The Son of Glory interjected, "This man is made of *terra firma* a solid substance far inferior to anything in this Kingdom, but I will place My Kingdom within him."

Pounding drums!

"Man will one day worship with the song of Heaven inherent to the nature of the Son of Glory," said the Almighty.

Trumpet fanfare!

"I will change his earthen body and transform him into a true living creature that will worship Us," confirmed the Son of Glory.

The Godhead agreed unanimously that the Son of Glory should be born of the seed of mankind. It was imperative for the Son of Glory to show His man-side to the inhabitants of earth. He would settle the matter once and for all that man could choose to carry out the will of the Godhead, unlike Lucifer who rebelled.

***

The Godhead communicated with each Other by Their ability to think-talk.

All thinking simultaneously...

The Holy One: "The Son of Glory will sacrifice His life for mankind."

The Son of Glory: "I will give My life a living sacrifice."

The Almighty: "I will give My Son a ransom for many."

Then They turned and looked at the sea of angels, all transfixed awaiting Their next announcement and by Their sheer will, the Godhead placed Their thoughts in the great multitude, never uttering a word.

"Why should the Son of Glory give His life for this creature made of inferior matter?" the angels asked disparagingly, with one unified voice.

Pounding drums...trumpet fanfare...a blast of wind! Whoooosssh!

The Godhead resolvedly declared,

In unison...

"There is only one way whereby man can be saved and that must be through the death, burial, and resurrection of the Son of Glory."

Enough said...
Silence.

The plan of the Godhead was underway.

The Son of Glory would be taken to the highest place of the mountain called Golgotha, which means, place of the skull, and it would serve as a reminder of the bitter memory of that day on the Mount of the Congregation.

On Golgotha, the true worshipers would be born. Unlike Lucifer, these worshipers would choose to worship with their whole heart, will, and emotions. In the same manner, the Son of Glory would die for them with His whole heart, will, and emotions.

The Almighty spoke of a death device called the cross. He held up two of the holy scepters crisscrossing them in the middle, forming a cross. It cast a great shadow that extended beyond the multitude as the radiant light from the Godhead shined illustriously. In the center of the two scepters, a glistening starburst appeared. After He replaced the scepters in their rightful place, the shadow lingered. The radiant light from the Godhead had burned a translucent positive image in the atmosphere. Only this shadow did not have a dark cast as a terrestrial shadow; it had a lovely amber glow. The soft, hazy shadow was forever etched into that place and would serve as a figurative bridge connecting the two worlds: Heaven and earth.

He spoke of nails, which would penetrate the lovely hands and feet of the Son, and gave a detailed description of a powerful substance called blood.

This priceless substance is an elegantly vibrant red color, much like the Son of Glory's throne. It has the power to eradicate the vilest of transgressions. For mankind would also fall away as did Lucifer, the entire species would become offended, nevertheless, this blood would be the reparation for the sins of man.

He said the precious liquid would flow from the Son's hands and feet and would provide atonement for the fallen nature of mankind.

He further explained that He and the Holy One would be forced to turn Their backs at the sight of the Son of Glory being crucified. They, too, would be reminded of the beautiful times reminiscent of days gone by. Each member of the Godhead would suffer in an attempt to restore worship to the Kingdom.

After, the crucifixion the Holy One would take the place of the Son of Glory and, willingly, live among the chaos of earth. His would be the pain of enduring thousands of human years among disorder. For He is order personified.

The angels began reminiscing when all would gather at the mount to worship.

To magnify...

To extol the greatness of the Godhead.

They reminisced how the Holy One would see to all the details of each gathering.

Order had always been the realm of the Kingdom, and the Holy One had set out to restore it.

The Almighty discussed the plans to save mankind and it became too painful for Him to continue. So, the Son of Glory completed His speech. The Godhead worked and flowed together in total, uninterrupted agreement supporting One Another, never in a competitive manner.

Trumpet fanfare...

"I must go and live among these mere mortals that they may have an occasion to see the glory of the Godhead," explained the Son of Glory.

***

...And for three days Heaven would remain completely silent.

Heaven would lay motionless. The sentinel silence would remain undisturbed until the Godhead announced a change in plans or decide to use someone other than the Son of Glory. Regardless, no one could utter a word.

Only the four creatures would continue their chanting, and that, by an internal telepathic convergence with the Godhead and with one another.

Because They were agreed!

...for Theirs is the honour, the glory, and the power, forever and ever, world without end!

***

Tat ta da da!

The Son of Glory continued, "For three days I will be laid up in a tomb allowing Lucifer to fall under a delusion, presumptuously thinking that he has defeated the Godhead."

Then, as if by an internal knowing, the Son of Glory humbly took His seat; and simultaneously, the Almighty rose from His throne...

Boomb!   Boomb!   Boomb!   Boomb!
Boomb!   Boomb!   Boomb!

Victoriously, He proclaimed with His majestic voice,

"On the third day after the silence, the Son of Glory will be resurrected! Then Lucifer will be stripped of the power that I have allotted him, and I will give man the power to take him underfoot!"

The angels began shouting. Some spun around in circles causing them to spiral up several feet into the air. Victorious chants could be heard from all over.

Pounding timpani drums...

"Then the Son of Glory will strip Lucifer of his power and confiscate the keys to the Kingdom."

Lucifer had taken the keys to the Kingdom with him upon his extirpation from Heaven.

More pounding drums...a rhythm is established...

Boomb boo-boom boom...

Boomb boo-boom boom...

"And then the Son of Glory will have defeated the dragon!"

Boomb boo-boom boom...

The angels unanimously cheered and shouted in cadence with the pounding drums,

Boomb boo-boom boom...
"Ha   lle   lu   jah!"
Boomb boo-boom boom...
"Ha   lle   lu   jah!"
Boomb boo-boom boom...
"Ha   lle   lu   jah!"

They created such a stir that the clouds rolled back, and the earth was made visible.

Looming in the distance a brawny, stout stallion majestically galloped to the platform enthronement. The Son of Glory rose from His throne and mounted on the handsome white steed that moments earlier was not and now was.

Then in a dazzling array of splendor the Son of Glory rode through the gaping porthole and He was resplendent! The horse's mane waved in the wind as he galloped effortlessly through the atmosphere.

This porthole was surrounded by a wall of light that did not allow the different variations of the darkness in the depths of space to penetrate it. The Son of Glory rode in splendorous light all the way to earth.

No human could behold the light beaming through this cylindrical passageway. Its exterior blended in with its surroundings by the superimposition of the background patterns blending into the foreground, which made it seem invisible. Each portion of the clouds in the background obstructed by the passageway was exactly replicated on the exterior of the passageway. It was a master illusion.

The angels flapped their wings and clapped their hands. They rose several feet into the air as their wings gave flight in response to their incessant flapping.

The ransom process had begun.

***

Before the gathering at the Mount of the Congregation could be concluded, the day's events supernaturally, in the twinkling of an eye, came to be.

In a few celestial moments, the Son of Glory had been born of a virgin, taken on the likeness of man, was tried, convicted, and then crucified.

Darkness covers the Heavens...
Lightening flashes...
The Almighty roars...
The Holy One weeps...
And the angels bow, lay prostrate, and cover their heads with their wings...
And once again...

DR. THOMAS MICHAEL

... Heaven was silent.

The Heavens were in a state of mourning. Without drawing from the earth's valuable resource of the sparkling, liquid matter, they cried. Without any help from the evaporation process the Almighty had established for them...

They wept.

They rolled.

They gushed.

They thundered; they flashed their lightening.

The Almighty created the Heavens as a covering for mankind, that is, the earthly Heavens because the Heavenly Heavens have always been; they came from deep within Him. The eternal Heavens were formed throughout the ages from the breath of His nostrils.

He had to provide protection for earth from the Heavenly Heavens because the brightness from His glory was too great, too marvelous for the *terra firma* to comprehend or conceive.

***

The Son of Glory lay in a solemn state. His suffering had come, not from the pain in His physical body, instead, His heart had been broken and shattered. His pain came because of the separation from His counterparts: The Almighty and the Holy One. Oh, the anguish and the torment. They had always been together; They had always been One.

Heaven was drowned in the bottomless silence that fills Heavenly habitations only once in an eternity.

In the timeless hours before dawn when the needs, wants, and wishes of the previous day were beginning to fade and those of the next day were not yet acknowledged, when the insensate species of the God-man floated inanimately between Heaven and earth; there the earth cried out in agony for its Inventor, its Designer.

The sub-kingdom fell under a deep trance. Birds in flight perched themselves; the skies became empty of their aerial movements.

In the deep, unexplored bush and forests of the world, animals ceased from their prowling. The lion and the adder's prowess were subject to the stillness of the moment. Plants drooped as they yielded their life-giving oxygen to the stiflingly motionless atmosphere.

The ant ceased its laboring, the cricket played his music no more and the sub-kingdom was subdued.

High atop a towering redwood tree, among the overabundant, numerous species of fowl, a lowly, insignificant sparrow, oblivious to the cataclysmic-all encompassing event, intoned her morning melody. Out of the gloomy sky above shone a single ray of light that pierced through the little bird's heart and with a telepathic message informed her of the saddened event. Her melody came to an abrupt stop. She reverently spread her delicate wings and, as if in slow motion, flew to the lowest part of the arborous shrine of silence and hid in the thick of the forest.

Somewhere beneath the many lithospheres of this mortal world, the earth quaked, shook, and churned. Subterranean volcanoes erupted and spewed out their lava in languished grief.

Mountains that had existed from the beginning of creation, deep in the bottomless, cavernous depths of the ocean were leveled flat, as they succumbed to their sorrow.

Canyons that were formed by rivers carving and etching their way to the sea constricted their passageways colliding one with the other forcing the water to explosively burst into the open air. Fault lines opened and closed with tremulous tremors.

His lifeless, resplendent body was placed in a cold, dark, clammy tomb. Sable shadows metastasized in sinister profusion within these dark walls made of lusterless, coarse stone.

From the beginning of time these walls had been formed, fashioned, and secured for this very purpose. They were the sole part of creation that had never seen the light of glory. They had remained in darkness and obscurity from the very beginning.

Amidst the lovely pleasantries in the grand earthly scheme there was a part that the Almighty did not touch. Out of this abyssal darkness and depravation of the life-giving source of the Godhead, it had created its own grotto. Buried within itself, within its own cryptic destiny, it burrowed out a chasm for the Savior of the world.

Other caverns, subjugated by the forces of earth, had burrowed out their own cavities in the landscape of earth's arid and barren terrain. These were decorated with stalagmites and stalactites, creating ornamentations of unexplored beauty, only to be relished some day when man would search out the secrets of the deep.

In the Kingdom, the Almighty and the Holy One had retreated to Their chambers. The great iridescent doors remained ajar. They had always closed, like a vault, of their own will; but now, it was as though they knew Someone was missing; Someone had not graced their entryway as normal. They remained unclosed because they refused to shut out the missing member.

The two members of the Godhead escaped to the Secret Place, turning Their backs to the cries of the Son of Glory.

"Eli, Eli, lama shevecatani!" shouted the Son of Glory as He gave up His last breath on the cross. That is to say, "My God, My God, why have You made a bachelor of Me?" The perfect union; the marriage between the Godhead had been disrupted by the transgression of man. The divorcement from His two beloveds was more than He could bear, and the Son of Glory gave up His Spirit.

Utter silence...

The natural physiological process of the human body to shut out pain had anesthetized the physical pain of the cross. **His greatest pain had been the result of an acute awareness that high above Him, in the chambers of the Godhead, the Almighty and the Holy One stood alone...without Him.**

He was the Dreamer, the Castle Builder. The eternal rhapsody They had enjoyed for ages had been devastated. Oh, how it had pained Him. The full embodiment of His thoughts, will, and emotions were toward the Partners and Their pure and holy desire was toward Him.

His last breath signified the disbandment of His union with the never before separated Godhead.

Some of the angels near the porthole peered through and watched in dreadfulness as the Son of Glory cried out in anguish to be rescued.

But there would be no rescue.

There would be no substitute.

There would be no ram caught in the thicket as with Abraham and his son, Isaac.

This was His purpose, and that to destroy the works of darkness. So, He willingly gave His life.

Holy silence...

Selah!

Then, in one hallowed moment, the Holy One mounted a chariot of clouds headed toward planet earth, and rode on the wings of His four winds.

Multiple horses galloping in the wind.

Wind blowing from the North, the South, the East and the West.

The angels whispered softly as He rode past them; "Who makes the clouds His chariot, Who rides on the wings of the wind? Holy One, Holy One, Holy One; the Holy One is He."

Holiness...
Perfection descending...
Down...
Down...
Further...
Still further...

The closer the Holy One got to the place where the Son was laid, His heart raced with utopian expectation.

He arrived in splendor and majesty; a host of angels had been sent before Him and rustled about in anticipation.

The chariot of clouds evaporated as the Holy One unfettered by the laws of gravity and solid matter materialized on the other side of the sealed tomb.

Two soldiers stood guarding the site where the body of the Son of Glory, now referred to as Jesus, the Christ, lay. They looked at each other as the Holy One passed in front of their limited earthly sight. Although they could not see the Holy One, still, they sensed His glory and stood in apprehension as His awesome, fearful presence passed by them. The angels surrounding the tomb chortled as the two guards looked here and there with eyes bugged trying to figure out what it was they did not see.

The Holy One hovered over His partner; His heart filled with pure grief, pure love, pure desire for the Member of the Godhead. Eye to eye, nose to nose, face to face He drifted gently over the image of Himself. In the privacy of this secluded moment, the Holy One manifested His image by embodying the person of the Son of Glory. **He took in a deep breath and in an instant the expired body of the Son of Glory was filled with the breath of Heaven.** Clouds billowed and filled the groin vault and cavernous transepts of this makeshift cathedral.

The amalgamation of both the Holy One and the Son of Glory in the same form created a synergistic, sovereign energy that produced a light more brilliant than all the solar systems combined. Its beaming brightness produced an explosive, voluminous sound that catapulted the heavy stone several yards away. The clouds that had filled the Godly grotto exploded with joy as the stone gave way. They scampered and billowed.

Rising...

Rising higher...

Rising higher and higher and higher until at last They had reached the splendor of glory, and They joined the triumph of the skies.

Hallelujah!

Hallelujah!

Hallelujah!

The two soldiers, who stood watch, were entranced and stupefied by the aura that had seeped out from the cave as the Holy One and the Son of Glory corroborated with One Another. The two became as dead men because the glory was too much, too splendid, and too marvelous for their meager eyes to behold.

The Holy One kissed the Son with the kiss of worship.

And the power of the Godhead shone with the brilliance of millions times millions of stars, suns, and moons combined. Heaven's silence was broken; and in celebratory shouts, the angels cheered once again in their, now, familiar language of worship,

"Hallelujah!"

"Hallelujah!"

"Hallelujah!"

The Son of Glory was resurrected!

He presented Himself to one of His devout followers who had come to the grave to tend His human body. And, then, the Holy One whisked Him away in an instant. Upon the chariot of clouds They rode, angels heralding Their arrival. They rode over the

Place of Crossing, beyond the Crystal Sea, around the great Mountain of the West, above the great River of Life and, then, to the Mount of the Congregation. And there, the Son of Glory stood where Lucifer once ruled and produced the song of Heaven.

He stood atop the summit and lifted His glorious hands and out of Him came the song of the human beings from earth.

It was the song of the redeemed...

The song of the saved...

The song of the Blood...

The song of true worship!

The angels cried: Holy, holy, holy, Lord God Almighty, Who was, Who is, and is to come!

He wore a mantle with a train that covered the entire mountain. It was made of fine, delicately woven silk. This silk was not produced by little silkworms; instead, it was loomed from a raw material found only on the mountains of Heaven. The luxurious damask print was a deep hue of royal blue with gold and silver cording that wrapped around the entire perimeter of the robe. His ephod was made of linen in the same royal blue color with textiles embroidered on the chest like a breastplate. It was bejeweled with exquisite gemstones of sardius, topaz, carbuncle, emerald, sapphire, diamond, ligure, agate, amethyst, beryl, onyx and jasper; twelve different stones in all, set in pure gold. Gold and silver alternating fringe hemmed the border, and bells intertwined throughout. A sash of gold with bells at each end was tied around His waist. Pomegranates in sapphire-blue, purple-passion, and sacred-scarlet colors were woven among the damask design. He majestically walked down the backside of the mount toward the thrones. His train filled the place and supernaturally lifted from Him and rose high above the thrones and disintegrated into beautiful gold and silver sparkling dust. And it fell on all who were there, and they were in awe.

After being reunited with the Almighty, the Son of Glory returned to earth and appeared to His disciples; and for the first time, man saw the glory of the Godhead.

Heaven came down, and the glory of God covered the earth, and the earth was forever transformed.

The Son of Glory continued on the earth for a few more celestial moments; and when His purpose had been fulfilled, He ascended a final time unto the Almighty and situated Himself upon His ruby throne at the right hand.

He carried a duteous devotion in His heart for the creatures He had left behind who autonomically pursued and craved the glory due to the lack of His presence. He would forever intercede on their behalf.

After the Son of Glory had revealed glimpses of the eminent essence of the Godhead to mankind, man's internal yearning drove Him to passionate pursuit.

He turned and looked at the Almighty, who gave Him a reassuring nod, for He perceived the heaviness in His heart. The Son of Glory empathically felt what the Holy One was feeling when the Son of Glory had traveled far below.

The thought of the sensitive, pure, and Holy One returning to earth in His stead was all too painful. The Almighty and the Son both turned and looked toward the diamond throne.

It was empty.

The Godhead would be forced to exist without the Holy One until, one day, when the chosen, the elect had been persuaded to worship in spirit and in truth.

The Son of Glory had paid the price; and now, the Holy One would prepare man's heart for true worship and veneration.

...for Theirs is the honour, the glory, and the power, forever and ever, world without end!

From the obscurity of earth came a sound familiar only to Heaven.

It was the song of true worship.
The Holy One, now positioned on earth, reached up through the worship of those who had chosen to offer their song of adoration.
They sang of the mercies of the Lord.
They sang of the goodness of the Lord.
They sang their song of love and gratitude.
It was the pure song of worship.
Man had conceived the seed of worship through the Holy One abiding in him.
Once again, the Kingdom heard the beautiful sounds of music.

...for Theirs is the Kingdom, the honour, the glory, and the power, forever and ever, world without end! Amen.

NINE

The Torment of Offense

The Torment of Offense

"Who opposes and exalts himself so proudly and insolently against and over all that is called God or that is worshiped, [even to his actually] taking his seat in the temple of God, proclaiming that he himself is God." (II Thessalonians 2:4 AMP) This is referring to the secret power of lawlessness - the offense.

Offense is an internal problem rather than an external one. It is the condition of one's heart.

The pain of losing a loved one is a condition in your heart not in your flesh. The anguish is not something you remedy with two aspirins; it is an inner aching.

Offense has a torment that is not visible to the flesh,

but gnaws away at the inner being until the soul becomes fragmented.

I recently had a bout with a condition called trigeminal neuralgia. It is known as the most excruciating pain known to medicine. It is a malady, which creates pain on either side of your face with electrical like shocks. To look at me, there are no visible signs of sickness; but, on the inside, I feel the torment of a relentless pain. When I am in the midst of one of these episodes, I am unable to function.

Offense has an unseen anguish that amplifies the remotest detail of hurt and pain. And like the neuralgia, it creates dysfunctional people. They walk around with fragmented souls, incapable of maintaining relationships at any level, affecting, even, their relationship with the Lord.

Can you imagine something evil sitting in the middle of your worship service? You are probably saying, "Not in my church."

You may argue that you have not observed any diabolical activity taking place in your fellowship; but, unfortunately, it is there.

"And the man of lawlessness (sin) is revealed, who is the son of doom (of perdition), Who opposes and exalts himself so proudly and insolently against and over all that is called God or that is worshiped, [even to his actually] taking his seat in the temple of God, proclaiming that he himself is God. For the mystery of lawlessness (that hidden principle of rebellion against constituted authority) is already at work in the world, [but it is] restrained only until he who restrains is taken out of the way. And then the lawless one (the antichrist) will be revealed and the Lord Jesus will slay him with the breath of His mouth and bring him to an end by His appearing at His coming. The coming [of the lawless one, the antichrist] is through the activity and working of Satan and will be attended by great power and with all sorts of [pretended] miracles and signs and delusive marvels - [all of them] lying wonders - And by unlimited seduction to evil and with all wicked deception for those who are perishing (going to perdition) because they did not welcome the Truth but refused to love it that they might be saved. Therefore God sends upon them a misleading influence, a working of error and a strong delusion to make them believe what is false." (II Thessalonians 2:3b-4a, 7-11 AMP)

It is vital that you fully comprehend this passage in order to recognize the power of offense. Allow me to make a shift in standard doctrine to prove that this antichrist is not some public figure as many are prone to believe.

Over the years, I have heard many opinion-based, theological assertions that the antichrist is going to be a man. I remember hearing that Henry Kissinger, the former Secretary of State, who served under President Nixon, was the antichrist. I have even heard Christians speculating that, perhaps, Elvis Presley would come back as the antichrist. Sometimes, I am amazed at the interpretations of Scripture some Christians entertain.

The book of Daniel speaks of the antichrist spirit coming to wear out the saints. I have heard the theory; if you become too busy, the antichrist is trying to wear you out.

The true workings of an antichrist spirit is to divert your attention from Christ-the Living Word. Your busyness may very well be a distraction to your relationship with Christ.

Verse four of this passage in II Thessalonians says this spirit opposes and exalts himself against anything that goes by the name of God, even to the point of making himself comfortable in the house of God.

There is not a devil in hell that can sit through an anointed service without being tormented to the point of exorcism.

Yet, offense sets itself up in the house of God proclaiming that he himself is God. **This spirit is obviously familiar with worship and has found a way to masquerade itself in people's lives.**

Offense is a brazen, selfish, self-centered spirit. Verse seven says, "For the mystery of lawlessness (that hidden principle of rebellion against constituted authority)..." The Amplified Bible refers to it as a "hidden principle of rebellion". This does not refer to one particular person as the antichrist rather a principle.

One of the main problems in Christianity is people do not want to submit to the organized system and protocol of authority. Few people truly submit to one another whether by marriage or by spiritual authority. That sounds like rebellion to me.

It is time we stopped trying to cosmetically improve the look of rebellion by dressing it up with the garment of excuses. *"Well, I am just different. I have a different calling. I have a different anointing. I'm not from the old school. I'm called to be independent."* There are numerous divisions and disagreements amidst the Body of Christ, and the root spirit is rebellion, which is seated in offense. Simply and plainly put; it is rebellion, anarchy, and lawlessness, which are a direct result and by-product of offense.

A secret power is at work right now. It can work in the heart of someone who has served Christ longer than you or I have been alive because it can trick a person. It looms its web of deception ever so craftily. Its silent caustic schemes are carried out with precision, knowing that everyone has an achilles heel and can be brought down swiftly.

This passage found in II Thessalonians is very direct when it speaks of this delusion. Offense leads to lawlessness, which renders the individual powerless to forces beyond their control. Some of these forces are governed and sent by God. This passage poignantly states that God, Himself, will place a strong delusion over many and they will believe a lie.

Have you ever been around someone who has a problem lying, who is so convincing they believe his or her own lies? After a season of ignoring the promptings of the Holy Spirit and quenching Him, an individual's conscience becomes seared. God turns them over to a grand delusion.

The Apostle Paul writes about people becoming deceived regarding the return of Christ. Many were under the impression that Christ had scheduled His return during their time. It is quite evident that Christ did not find His bride ready for rapture in that day.

It is delusional for our generation, with it's rampantly out of control sinful nature, to think that Christ has reserved His grand return for this hour. I would love, more than anything, to believe that Christ has scheduled His return for our age. However, the Bride has not put on the garments of worship - the Bride's wedding dress.

WISDOM PRINCIPLE: WORSHIP IS THE VEIL OF THE BRIDE.

Only worship could cover the inherent character flaws of our human nature. Under the veil of worship, we are beautiful before the Bridegroom.

Have you ever seen an ugly bride? Probably not. There is no such thing as an ugly bride. The veil she wears over her face covers any blemish beyond her control. After the ceremony of marriage, her looks become inconsequential because the Bridegroom's love sees beyond the veil. Likewise, our, yet, unchanged blemishes will be covered, and when we see the

Bridegroom, "we shall be changed in the twinkling of an eye".

Brides spend countless months in preparation for their wedding day. The special attention to hair, skin, and nails must be scheduled down to the final hours. The preparation involves a ritual of physical pampering, all too often, leaving unresolved issues with their fiancés and family members to fate.

The Church has pampered the outward man leaving the unseen, unresolved matters of the heart to fate. What will be the fate of a people who fail to recognize a God who desires, more than anything, fellowship and true worship?

It is time for the bride of Christ to go beyond the veil and enter into an intimate relationship with the Lord.

In the Old Testament teaching of the temple, the whole purpose of the tabernacle was about worship. The priest would go in once a year to offer up the sacrificial elements of worship on behalf of the people. Their mission in the Holy of Holies was to intercede on behalf of the people. However, intercession in this sense was not about petition. Many believers have mistaken time in the secret place as a time for petitioning.

Believers have long interpreted prayer as petitioning. The original translation of the word prayer is worship. Our prayers to God should not be a long list of needs, rather a long list of declarations of God's greatness.

WISDOM PRINCIPLE: GOD WILL BE WHAT YOU DECLARE HIM TO BE.

The whole purpose of the Levitical Priesthood was to establish worship in the temple. Worship is the passageway to the presence of God. From the very beginning, God intended for man to dwell in the presence of the Lord. Eden means the presence of God. God put Adam in His presence to dwell.

God is looking for worshipers who will worship Him in spirit and in truth. It is time to go past the veil through true worship and move into habitation. The Holy of Holies is not some casual meeting place it is the habitation of the presence of God and His bride.

Escape the torment of offense for the sake of staying behind the veil of worship; it is your only hope. Become acutely aware of the tormenting traits of this evil entrapment. Do not be caught on your wedding day unprepared without your veil.

WISDOM PRINCIPLE: WORSHIP IS THE GARMENT THAT COVERS OUR DISORDER AND QUALIFIES US FOR INTIMACY WITH GOD.

Once again, the problem lies not in cleaning up the outward, rather, in dealing with the hidden secrets of the heart. There will always be a war between the flesh and the spirit.

Naturally, this does not mean there is liberty to do as one pleases. The Apostle Paul wrote, "Shall we continue in sin that grace may abound? God forbid!" Still, many believers struggle bringing their flesh into submission to the Word of God. Outward sin is an indicator of an internal problem.

WISDOM PRINCIPLE: YOUR FLESH CANNOT DO WHAT YOUR SPIRIT-MAN OR SUBCONSCIOUS-MAN IS UNWILLING TO DICTATE!

How does one keep from fulfilling the desires of the flesh? Get the inside right, and the flesh will follow.

Believers, often, have problems with their emotional

foundations, which result in spiritual foundation damage.

If your own home had foundation problems, would you allow the problem to persist? Your house would eventually fall!

WISDOM PRINCIPLE: EMOTIONAL PROBLEMS ARE COLLECTED OFFENSES CREATING A NEGATIVE MEMORY.

Unless the foundation is repaired, the structure will continue to deteriorate.

Jesus also stated in one of the gospels that it is impossible to keep from becoming offended. Each one of us encounters daily areas where we might become offended. You become angry with someone; that is an offense.

While the offense is still in the realm of your mind, you are able to intelligibly deal with it. When it moves from the realm of your mind into your heart, you then require a deliverer.

The torment of estrangement from people God has assigned to your life can be agonizing.

What can separate you from the love of God?

According to the Scripture, nothing can or ever will. While nothing can separate you from God's love, your choices can separate you from His presence. The greatest torment of offense is isolation. Isolation from God's presence remains the greatest torment of all.

I mentioned in a previous chapter the demoniac of Gadara. This man represents more than just a couple of thousand demons wanting to enter into a herd of swine. He was known for the company he kept. He lived in a cemetery and found more comfort among the dead than among the living.

His life was out of control; he was completely lawless. No one could tell him what to do; he was quite reprehensible.

How does a person know when anger progresses into offense? It is when one has denied the promptings of the Holy Spirit to forgive an individual or a fateful event.

When offense moves into the heart, much like this oppressed man from Gadara, people run around naked and unashamed of their actions. When you refuse to forgive someone, while it is still in the power of your mind to choose to forgive, the eventual outcome is always offense.

Offense creates a state of mind that opposes any type of authority, whether natural or spiritual. The individual runs naked and unashamed of actions and reactions. Everyone around him can see his condition, but he is the last to discover the secret of his misery.

The demoniac ran around naked without even realizing his condition. He had cut himself off from his family, his friends, and from God.

WISDOM PRINCIPLE: ISOLATION IS THE FIRST PHASE OF OFFENSE.

Self-mutilation was a part of this man's daily ritual. So it is for the offended one, who unknowingly cuts himself off from his own individuality by removing golden and divine connections from his life.

The torment of offense resonates loudest in the seclusion from those whom God has assigned to your life. It becomes a matter of life and death.

WISDOM PRINCIPLE: THE BITTER ROOT OF OFFENSE IS A MATTER OF LIFE AND DEATH.

The demoniac had come to a place where the demons within him wanted to destroy him completely. Offense relentlessly gnaws away at the soul of its prey until it becomes all-consuming. If it is not dealt with, it can ravage through every relationship until its victim is left completely alone.

When an individual reaches this level of offense, not only do they seek isolation, but now it becomes necessary for the individual to be quarantined. Others around him must be wary of his venomous words, which can become caustic and deadly.

I just received a call from a girl whose sister has been offended for many years. She has held a grudge against their mother because she was birthed at home and her siblings were birthed in hospitals. She has decided to disown her mother and entire family in her adult years because of this offense. The venomous effects of her offense have affected another sibling, and he, too, has disowned the family in support of her offense.

I heard someone say, "God gives you a family to prepare you for your enemies."

No matter how strong your love for an individual, offense can deteriorate even the deepest love.

What if, suddenly, you found yourself without the ones you care for the most; can you imagine being torn away from them?

The torment of isolation, the lost time with them, and their absence would be inconceivable.

Yet, millions allow offense to rip their relationships apart numbed to the tormenting consequences. Culpability is cast away; the blame is placed on a scapegoat, and the cycle of unforgiveness begins. Conflict becomes the method for coping with relationships and the breeding ground for disparaging thoughts of loneliness.

WISDOM KEY: WHEN OFFENSE WALKS IN, LOVE WALKS OUT.

When love walks out, scorn and denigration walk in, and love becomes eclipsed with judgmental legalism.

This is one of the characteristics of lawlessness. You begin to judge everyone around you based on your self-right-eousness. When you move into a state of super-spirituality, where you feel you are qualified to judge others because you are superior, you have come under delusion. This is a danger-ous place to be because you have subjected yourself to the judg-ment of God.

When private conviction becomes public doctrine, you have moved into a judgmental attitude. Your offended spirit seeks to bring everyone under your personal convictions in an attempt to justify your inability to carry out those same convic-tions.

These kinds of people go around preaching their dogma to anyone and everyone striving to eclipse their deep-rooted offenses. They boast of their good deeds while hiding their misdeeds.

Offense is like a chameleon changing colors according to its environment. The offended one adapts to the nature of those with whom it can vent, endeavoring to justify his or her actions.

Offense is a multifaceted offender. It can take the pain of bereavement over the loss of a loved one and turn it into bit-terness toward life itself.

My wife's grandmother lived much of her life in negativity with a cynical attitude. She watched her sister burn to death as a child and was never the same. She never saw the sun shine again because of her inability to accept the sorrows of life. The death of her sister became an offense against life and, ultimately, against God.

Perhaps, you are thinking, she was a mean-spirited old lady; when in fact, she was kind, loving, and gentle. Yet, her kindheartedness always had a pleasureless aftertaste because offense makes the kindest deeds of its victims a source for manipulation. "I give you something, now you owe me something later." Offense makes you self-centered and everything revolves around you.

One of the most tormenting issues with offense is after the storm of bitterness, revenge, and rebellion are over you are left alone and lonely. Loneliness can be as lethal as a toxic drug. You do not know you are committing a slow suicide until it is almost too late. A person delighting in the euphoria of drugs only desires the immediate satisfaction unaware of its damaging effects.

Offense can take the temporal anguish of divorce and turn it into a lifetime of revenge. It can cause the divorcée to live life from a slanted, affronted perspective. Every relationship engaged from that point becomes the target of a ravenous, dangerous culprit fiercer than the enticement of a Jezebel. No longer do love and romance have room to run free; in their place, fear of rejection and revenge move in.

A woman who has suffered the ravaging shame of rape can become offended for the rest of her life. Male figures take on the form of monsters, and the cycle of hate towards men is initiated. In many instances, offense gives way to the ungodly entrapment of homosexuality.

Victims of incest can become traumatized to the point of

never enjoying a healthy, sexually active marriage. The offense of trauma can be just as damaging as that of anger, bitterness, and revenge.

I have known women whose husbands have abandoned them, and they have grown cynical and bitter. They are incapable of recognizing their condition because of the pain of offense.

The list goes on and on and, seemingly, never ends. The torment of offense is like a gruesome, festering sore that never heals.

There are people who have endured the suffering of cataclysmic world events. People who have survived world wars and times of famine find themselves losing their battle against offense. They view everything from a sense of loss and hoard as much as they can, all the while, shutting out good opportunities and good people from their lives.

A person who has suffered the loss of a loved one and refuses to accept that death is a part of the sequence of life has the same potential of becoming offended. When the pain of their loss remains a shrouded untouchable topic, chances are they will end up with a deep seeded offense. Obviously, the pain of death is a natural, justified emotion; no one expects the bereaved to think any differently. Yet, their offense is so deep that even the victim has difficulty recognizing the deep offense. They have trouble with their emotions, dealing with relationships, and seldom ever admit that they have a problem.

In many cultures, the grief over the death of a loved one is manifested through external expressions of pain and loss for the departed. They are encouraged to grieve publicly without shame in whatever manner they deem acceptable. Some have been known to lament over the casket with loud wailings of sorrow.

In our culture, we are taught never to show emotion,

often leaving the bereaved to deal with the pain and offense of the death for a later time. Commonly, that grief is never dealt with, and the cycle of offense ensues.

Of course, in some cases, these same people with demonstrative displays of grief fail to come out of their mourning and enter into a wager with offense where the victim always loses out.

I mentioned earlier that emotional instability is a collection of unresolved offenses. The longer an embittered individual eludes feelings of hatred, revenge, and offense: the deeper the root of offense grows. Jesus explained with a parable, "But he that received the seed into stony places, the same is he that heareth the word, and anon with joy receiveth it; Yet hath he not root in himself, but dureth for a while: for when tribulation or persecution ariseth because of the word, by and by he is offended." (Matthew 13:20,21)

This passage clearly states that if someone is offended, no matter how much of the Word of God they receive, it has no lasting effect. When they are subjected to difficult times, they become offended at the Word because offense is already resident in their hearts.

That is a frightening thought and quite sobering, yet, straight from the Word of God. You cannot argue the Word; you either agree with it and reap the benefits, or you disagree and reap the consequences.

Perhaps, you are thinking we could just lay hands on people and set them free from the spirit of offense.

To reiterate what I have said over and over, offense is a choice! It is a spirit that you choose to embrace. It does not have power over God's elect.

The individual must choose to admit his offense and repent.

The Word works for them that work it.

The only help you can offer an offended person is to pray that God will quickly bring His loving correction upon them and safely lead them back to the fold. There is only one way out of offense, and that is through Godly correction. A person either submits to Godly authority and stays free from offense or chooses the vile spirit resulting with the mandatory correction from God.

Are you dealing with unforgiveness and offense in your heart? Quickly repent, ask forgiveness, and release it. Meditate on the Scriptures, and receive your deliverance. Jesus simply used the deliberating power of His Word to deliver those who were oppressed with devils. (Matthew 8:16)

The Word of God is sharper than any two-edged sword and can set you free today!

***

Tori was the perfect wife.

She honoured her husband, loved her children, served in her church; and, yet, found herself entangled in the trap of **The Secret.** It furtively wove a web of offense masqueraded by good works leaving her to wonder if she would ever be free from its tight embrace.

❧

The Betrayal

❧

The Betrayal

Victoria married the man of her dreams. He was tall, dark, and handsome with one of those Marlboro-man mustaches. His nose was a bit on the large side, but his rugged, good looks camouflaged it well. His suave personality only added to his charm. They met in a nightclub when they were in college, and it was love at first sight.

Tori, as those closest to her called her, was a fiery, outspoken type personality. Her family and friends had their doubts about the kind of man who could handle such a fireball. Their courtship lasted a few months, and Tori was completely smitten. Stephen had a way of getting her to do anything he wanted.

She was in love.

She had found her prince charming.

Although she felt secure in her relationship with her husband, there was something suspicious about her prince charming. Stephen's past was a constant agitation to her uncertainties. He was a hopeless flirt.

Eight years into their marriage, she began to sense an emptiness in her spirit that she could not explain. It was a penetrating loneliness. Something was missing from her fairy tale fantasy. She had everything she could ever want; a great husband, a healthy, beautiful child, a nice home, a new car, and a fantastic job. So why was she so unhappy? Why was she so empty? This marked the beginning of her search for self-fulfillment.

Her quest for answers led her to dig deep into her spiritual self. She read books on transcendental meditation, mysticism, and any other spiritual reading she could get her hands on. Still empty and desperate for something to fulfill the deep void in her inner person, Tori agreed to attend a prayer meeting at the request of one of her neighbors.

Someone had convinced her earlier to watch the video, "Left Behind", and it had made quite an impression on her.

Tori loved the relaxed atmosphere and the sincere worship she experienced that evening at the prayer meeting.

Before long, she was attending the small full gospel church regularly with her husband and neighbor.

Stephen was a passionate man and quickly found himself devoted to his newfound faith. His faithfulness soon afforded him a promotion, and he was asked to join the worship team.

Tori often felt insecure about Stephen's behavior with certain women in the church but never allowed her insecurities to be voiced. There was always a fear of what people might say if they found out her marriage was not perfect. Stephen traveled several days out of the month and that only added to her worries.

Two years later, she was elated to learn that she was pregnant once again, after patiently waiting for six years for her second child. Tori rubbed her stomach as she learned she would have another baby. She thought, surely, the arrival of a new baby would bring a greater fulfillment in life, and it did. Life was wonderful!

The fairy tale continued to blossom, unbeknown to Tori; a dark enchantress called offense was looming its way into her heart.

Stephen, too, was ecstatic about the new baby. He was hoping for a boy. He had had dreams of the two of them playing ball. Although their first baby was not a boy, Stephen had not been disappointed. The little bundle of joy wrapped him tight around her little finger in no time. She was her daddy's girl. Tori used to watch the two of them as they wrestled around on the floor hours at a time.

"You're going to make a tom-boy out of her, Stephen." Tori would say.

But, oh, how she loved to watch them. It was truly a wonderful life!

Tori remembered the day her world came crashing down around her. She was confronted with a difficult situation and was thrust into a nightmare unlike she had ever experienced. Had it not been for the strength she had come to depend on from her relationship with the Lord, she would not have made it.

Sitting in church one hot summer Sunday morning, Tori felt a strange uneasiness in her spirit. This pregnancy was taking its toll on her. She gained a few pounds more with this baby than with her first pregnancy. She was experiencing morning sickness almost every day of her first two trimesters. This was not an easy time in her life. Perhaps, that was the unsettled feeling she felt.

The worship service was beautiful as usual. The pastor

delivered a wonderful message about trusting the Lord. His words were still ringing in her ears by the close of the service; and yet, she could not resolve herself to relax and *trust the Lord*. Her spirit was sorely vexed; and somehow, she knew that something was terribly wrong.

Stephen did not say a word during their drive to church that morning; and, still, had said very little at the close of the service. He was unusually quiet.

Tori contemplated, "Could he be feeling the same thing I am? Is something going to happen to my new baby?"

The drive home seemed longer and somewhat dreary. There was a lovely park with rows and rows of red tulips sprouting above a bed of purple lantana and flowers of all kinds. The tulips were beginning to wither; it was the beginning of summer. There was a fabulous fountain in the center, with birds perched upon it, basking in the sun and drizzling water they cupped in their tiny mouths all over their colorful feathers. Stephen and Tori had driven past this same park every Sunday and Wednesday to and from church. It was like a Garden of Eden in the middle of American suburbia. She and Stephen took many walks together in this secret garden. Then Brianna came along, and the strolls in the park became a vanishing luxury. As did the days of sitting together on the cement benches feeding the pigeons stale bread from their pantry.

On one occasion, they prayed for a sign of their familial future. They wondered how many children the Lord would allow them to raise. Tori took a piece of bread and split it between her and Stephen. Like a ritual, they both tossed their portions of bread into the direction of the ever-hungry pigeons. Oh, how they laughed! The number of pigeons eating the morsels of bread would be the count of how many children they would have. Before the bread had even hit the ground, a swarm of 38 pigeons had landed. And that was no exaggeration; they had counted and verified their accounting twice. Laughing always made her feel so full of life.

Now there seemed to be a great distance between the two lovebirds, as they drove past the garden that no longer beckoned them because something inside of them had been taken away.

She felt so distanced from Stephen. The silence in their car was terribly disturbing. The rays from the sun piercing their way through the tinted windows reflected off the pen Tori held in her hand. It gleamed like the sharp edge of a knife. Her thoughts rambled in her head.

"If this were a knife I would just kill myself." She quickly regained her thoughts just before she formulated the rest of her mental picture. "I'll kill Steph..."

Tori's feelings of nervousness and uneasiness intensified as they drove into their garage that Sunday afternoon. Stephen had insisted on a front-entry garage for safety purposes when they had moved into their new home. He didn't want his beautiful bride driving in from the rear in the dark since he traveled quite extensively. Now, it seemed he could care less. He jumped out of the car, leaving Tori to tend with the stack of Bibles, books and notepads, along with the ice chest the youth department had borrowed for their car wash the previous week.

Tori sat in silence for a moment until the car became uncomfortably warm as the cool interior gave way to the summer heat. A bead of sweat had formed on her brow line; it trickled down into her eye and caused her to blink repeatedly; it became irritated and tears flowed. Was it the stinging of her makeup or were these tears of frustration? She stacked the Bibles and books on the ice chest and lifted it from the handles. Her hands were stretched to the maximum as the chest rested against her swollen stomach. One of the legal pads fell as she walked through the crowded laundry room from the garage into the kitchen. She left the notepad and decided to pick it up later when she collected the trash; Monday was trash day.

Stephen settled himself upstairs in the family room on his favorite recliner; Tori's parents had brought the chair over after the arrival of the first grandchild. Stephen sat back kicking his shoes off, grabbing the remote control for the television, and pushing back the recliner to a reclined position. He had these actions down to a fine art. It was all one fluid motion. Stephen's mind was so far away from the chair, the in-laws, and his pregnant wife. He was settled in for his Sunday afternoon nap.

Sleepy...
Very sleepy...

The big screen TV was going; a football game was under way. They had bought the surround sound package because that's what Stephen had wanted. He tried watching, but his eyes were heavy. The TV blurred, the sounds of the cheering crowd faded, and something came over him like a thick, heavy blanket.

Falling into a heavy sleep...

In the other room, Tori was feeling nauseous. Her mind was beginning to put things together.

Something was eating away at Stephen; instead of dealing with his emotions, he slipped into never-never land and fell into a deep sleep.

Asleep.

Stephen had grown quite fond of his new friends and newly acquired family at the church. Not to mention, all of his responsibilities that had knit him closely with the pastor and the leaders were an added bonus. Stephen used his relationships with the upper echelon of the church to make himself feel justified in his wrongdoing.

A hotel room on the beach, a spectacular view. The

woman of his dreams beside him, this is as good as it gets.

Stephen slipped off his jacket and changed his clothes and sported the youthful swimming trunks he had bought especially for their weekend getaway.

The love of his life came out of the dressing room dressed in a great looking bikini. She wore a silky, see-through swimsuit wrap that hugged her hips beautifully. Stephen stood in awe as he beheld the beauty of this marvelous creature. Vanessa slipped on her high heels and walked over to Stephen. It was like a dream...Wait, it was a dream...

He had met Vanessa at a casino in Vegas on one of his business trips.

He felt uneasy about his indiscretions even in his dream, but he was enjoying his flashback.

Vanessa meandered over to Stephen, her hair draped over the left side of her face as she cocked her head slightly.

Dreaming...

She placed her hands on Stephen's shoulders and looked into his eyes. In a flash, in a dream moment, the woman standing before him was Tori. Her eyes immediately flooded with tears, and the sexy woman in the bikini was now his 9-month pregnant wife. Stephen ran away in his dream-turned-nightmare episode.

Nightmare!

Stephen stirred in his sleep and mumbled something. Tori walked through the room where Stephen was resting. She moved stealthily and quietly so as not to wake him. She picked up his pants that hung from the side of the chair by the window. She heard Stephen whisper a name; she thought he said Clarissa, Varissa, or something like that. Tori disregarded the episode and continued with her Sunday duties.

Tori came into the kitchen after finally finishing her Sunday chores. She closed the door behind her and felt another wave of nausea coming over her. It was too late in the day to still be experiencing morning sickness. It must have been the heat of the Texas sun. She made her way to the sofa and sat. Rubbing her swollen tummy, she leaned back into the comfortable cushions of the sofa.

She and Stephen had purchased their first piece of furniture at Haverty's Fine Furniture just shortly after they were married. Stephen wanted a white couch, but she knew one day, children would be holding sippy-cups and jumping on the couch leaving their marks behind. She talked him into getting the blue one instead, with specks of darker blue and mauve. The pattern was great for hiding the wear and tear of family life. Not to mention, it was altogether more practical.

Tori winced. Already, another wave of nausea. She clasped her hands around her immense belly and took slow, deep breaths until the nausea subsided.

She ran her fingers through her short, spiked hair. She had cut her hair for easier care and convenience with the arrival of the new baby. She was feeling a bit wild and racy in those days, so she asked her hairdresser to add a touch of frost. She then proceeded to whack away at her long silky mane. Stephen had always liked her long hair. But he had agreed that the crop cut would be much more practical.

Brianna had taken out several chunks of her hair during her infant years.

The wild and feisty woman Stephen had married some years back had begun to mellow.

She nestled in closer into the decorative throw pillows on her favorite couch. She reached for one of the blue and mauve striped throw pillows and spotted her husband's briefcase. Her woman's intuition led her to look inside.

It was not unusual for her to rummage through her husband's things. She had gone through his pants and shirts for years, removing left over receipts and business cards while doing their laundry.

Tori was quite fastidious and maintained a very clean house for her husband. She was obsessed with doing things right and with integrity.

She opened the briefcase and another wave of nausea drained the color from her olive skin. She abruptly shut the lid and carried the case into the master bedroom. She felt a bit sneaky and suspicious; yet, she was compelled to look inside. She had a bad feeling about herself as if she were doing something terribly wrong. She shuffled through the papers and came across a brown envelope. Her hands began to shake; they became sweaty, and her heart missed a beat. She knew something evil, something wrong awaited her on the inside of the mysterious envelope.

A big tear formed in the corner of her eye. It trickled down the side of her cheek and into the crease of her frowning lips. The signs of aging were beginning to show on her face. The suspected affairs, the pregnancies, the housework, and full time job had taken its toll.

She flashed back to the time she had raced to the airport to pick Stephen up. She had unpacked his suitcase and found a shirt with a lipstick smudge. She confronted him about the issue.

"Check your lipstick; it's probably one of your own shades." Stephen replied.

Tori became emotional and insisted that it was not her lipstick, only to be riddled with accusatory questions. "What's wrong with you, why are you so suspicious? Is it the pregnancy, or should we find you a counselor?"

Anger, hurt, rejection...

She dumped the contents of the envelope onto the bed. She and Stephen had spent many blissful, romantic evenings together in this very bed. This is where baby Brianna had been conceived.

Another tear forced its way out of her other eye and opened up the floodgates. Her teary eyes focused on what she had suspected but had not allowed herself to consciously accept. There were pictures of another woman along with letters and sticky notes that said, "I love you," with the imprint of a woman's lips in scarlet red.

She ran to the bathroom and vomited, crying violently, feeling anger well up deep inside her heart.

Her mind raced a few months back to the previous Valentine's Day when Stephen came home with a Victoria's Secret negligee. She had caught him hiding it under the bed. He quickly chided her saying it was going to be a surprise for Valentine's Day. Stephen convinced her that he was trying to be romantic and was going to surprise her with something sexy for their special day after Valentine's Day, since he was called in to work that evening. Or so he said.

She picked up the garment and held it up to her body. She hadn't worn a sexy nightgown in months and certainly not one this skimpy. She struggled, pulling and tugging until the strained gown was finally over her swollen belly. Instead of it draping beautifully over her body, the satin that should have caressed her skin fit snugly around the shape of her now disfigured body. She felt unattractive as many pregnant women often do. Stephen wrapped his arms around her and chuckled lightly gently kissing her on the forehead.

"You look beautiful to me."

At the time, it never dawned on her that it might have been for another woman. He made her laugh saying he didn't know how to pick pregnant women's clothing. It was three sizes too small. She had believed his lies; and, now it was all in full color right before her very eyes.

She had sworn to herself that infidelity was one thing she would never tolerate. After the tears, came a resolve to never forgive him.

Her mind quickly raced back to the new teachings she had received from her newfound faith: forgiveness, no matter what the cost.

She was always good at confrontations, and this situation would call for the confrontation of confrontations.

A part of her wanted to run away and hide; another side wanted to commit murder and avenge herself. All the while her heart was saying, "Forgive him." She felt like Jekyl and Hyde. She was torn between right and wrong, between good and bad, and between doing what would bring gratification if there were such an emotion left in her.

It was Monday morning; her eyes were puffy from little sleep the night before. Stephen had left early that morning without waking her. She dressed and reported to her office for duty. She sat at her desk sipping her morning coffee. She looked at the inscription on the side of the cup; it was a big "I ♥ You" Stephen had filled with chocolate kisses two years prior, just because he loved her. She felt a twinge deep inside that reminded her how much she loved him. She pulled herself together, and the wild, independent Tori was called forth to deal with these brand new emotions. She would be nobody's fool.

Throughout the day, she flashed back at the wonderful times she and Stephen had shared together. The time they had jumped in their Volkswagen beetle bug and headed for the beach. How romantic that weekend had been. It was the same weekend the new baby was conceived.

There were many other memorable moments; but now, they were all gone. With one fail swoop of lust, a marriage, a solid marriage of several years was destroyed. It was over, as far as she knew. There was no way she would or could ever forgive him. The bitterness she had felt the day before was now masqueraded by a self-righteous attitude. She would do what she had to do. She had succumbed to the entrapment of offense.

From that point forward every thought she had about Stephen was seen from the slanted view of offense.

Although she was justified because of the hurt and rejection she had suffered, her heart became hardened and unforgiving. Life took on a different perspective. The truth was she had loved Stephen with everything in her, and they had shared marvelous, unforgettable times together, but she willed herself to forget all the good and remember only the bad.

When her husband came home late that afternoon, she confronted him with her findings. He tried to explain that the girl was simply a friend he had recently met.

Tori stared into his twitching eyes that took on an apathetic attitude. Her jaws clenched together, her lips pursed, her words forced their way out oozing with bitterness and revenge. "I want you out. I could never forgive you for what you have done." Something deep in her heart cringed as she spoke these words of condemnation.

After all, he had hurt her; he had done her so wrong. He deserved this and so much more.

Offense spread its evil talons and dug deep into her heart.

Later, he admitted that he and the woman in the pictures were having an affair. He apologized and promised to change. He begged and pleaded to be forgiven. He knew in his heart that the relationship with the woman he had been seeing was going nowhere. It had no qualities of a good, moral union because the woman worked in a strip club. No telling how many other men she was courting, all for the money, all for the special favors.

Tori loved Stephen for all the right reasons, and it was this true love that eventually helped her overcome her bitterness, or so she thought.

Tori decided to give him an ultimatum, hoping that he'd refuse, and they would both go their separate ways. The only way she would agree to stay in the marriage was for him to see a counselor. To her surprise he agreed.

A few weeks into the new agreement, she discovered he had been sleeping around with several other women and had been doing so for quite some time.

Tori found Stephen's little black book that was filled with names and numbers, which matched the phone bills she had requested from the phone company. He had always paid the bills, never allowing her to see them. She had outsmarted him and been slapped in the face with the startling truth of his deceptive doings.

Offense dug deeper.

Tori felt her baby kick on the side of her stomach as her nerves reacted to the news. She decided it would be best for her little girl and the baby who would soon arrive to stay put. Her decision was based solely on the needs of her children.

The feelings of revenge, hurt, and offense would be neatly tucked away and dealt with at another time.

She was desperate for some Godly counseling; and ran to her pastor who made a banal comment that all men who were not cared for at home eventually sought for what they needed elsewhere.

Tori felt a deep hatred for all men in that instant and left the church offended.

Offense dug deeper; beyond her emotions and into her heart; into her spirit.

She chose to forgive Stephen, at least for the moment but found it very difficult trusting him ever again. There had been many women before her who had forgiven and stayed with their husbands because of their children and/or for the money. Tori would stand by her man.

Their lives slowly resumed back to normalcy.

They found a way to deal with infidelity and soon found themselves busied beyond their problem. Tori never breathed a word of his indiscretions to the members of the the church; and soon, they were promoted to youth pastors and were appointed as elders a short while later.

The pain Tori felt was not so much over the infidelity but that she had been made a fool. She had taken great pride in her marriage and the ability to care for her man. The proud Tori had been brought low.

Offense spread its wings and reared its ugly head, making Tori feel justified for her bitterness and pride.

After 19 years of marriage, it seemed like their relationship was on solid ground. However, Tori had never truly forgiven Stephen. She had buried her anger and offense deep in her soul and covered it over with pride. She felt superior over Stephen; she had not cheated on him and had done nothing to destroy the trust between them. Yet, she had allowed offense and pride to rule her heart.

Even still, she was a devout wife and mother and did all she did with passion and commitment.

Months later, Stephen was spending much time on the road. He came home from one of his trips tired and stressed. He asked Tori for prayer.

He decided he had neglected his position as youth pastor, of which Tori did much of the planning and teaching; and consequently, resigned. A few months later, he decided to train someone to take over as worship leader and left that position as well.

Offense got what it wanted. It isolated Stephen and Tori.

She did not become suspicious, until he told her that he wanted to resign his eldership position because he felt that he and the pastor were no longer in agreement over certain issues. Tori retorted lightly, "My goodness, the next thing you'll be telling me is that you're walking out on me and the girls." Stephen stared coolly gazing out the window of their beautiful suburban home.

Surely, after all that they had been through and had overcome, he would never walk out on her.

Surely, the memories they had recreated since his indiscretions would override any difficulty that might arise. He responded with the last thing she would have expected,

"I've been thinking about the past 19 years...you and me. Maybe we made a mistake."

Her world came crashing down for the second time. She had never really gotten over the first devastation; and now, the rubble of her shambled life was piled even higher.

Offense dug its talons even deeper and she grew colder and harder.

"Are you seeing another woman?" Tori asked. He quickly denied it. She begged him to consider marriage counseling, but he refused. He didn't follow through with his counseling the first time; it was no surprise that he was disapproving of the idea now.

Tori was devastated. How could he do this a second time? A familiar feeling of rejection, shame, and anger intensified as she clenched her fists together in rage. Stephen turned and walked away with his head hung low.

Tori took the crystal vase they had received as a wedding gift from a wealthy couple from Stephen's work and hurled it across the room. It smashed against the glass étagère that held Stephen's prized rifle collection. The glass shattered and went flying across the room. Stephen's rifles collapsed one on top of the other. Scratched, dented, and mangled guns landed on the floor, like the rubble after a tornado's calamitous winds have wreaked their havoc.

Tori felt alone, afraid, and defeated. She had given him the best years of her life. How could she forgive him? Why should she have to forgive him?

Although she never blamed God for her situation, she was steeped in unforgiveness and bitterness and could not see it because she realized a few wrong choices from the past were now coming to fruition. She had married against her parents' wishes.

A few months later, after visiting with Stephen, the children told her they had met "daddy's friend", a very nice woman with four kids. Stephen was finally man enough and admitted he had left his family to be with this woman. Tori wanted a divorce and asked him to file. By the end of the year, the divorce was final.

Tori moved away unable to endure the pain and the shame of having to explain to all their mutual friends and church family why they were both leaving. The thought of people criticizing and judging her tormented her almost as much as her husband's betrayal.

Thoughts of everything she had lost because of his infidelity tormented her daily.

She carried the offense, and it haunted her day after day. She was no coward, but this situation was more than she could bear. She prayed for deliverance, but knew that she would have to forgive him with her heart not just with her lips, before she could feel a true inner peace.

On one of the occasions when picking up the children, she asked Stephen to forgive her for all that she had done to contribute to their break-up, especially for the bitterness and anger that she had harbored. He humbly accepted and was surprised that she felt a need to be forgiven.

Tori returned to her new home convinced that she would never again hold an offense toward anyone. She felt like a ton of weight had been lifted from her, and she was free.

Free from the weight of unforgiveness.
Free from the torment of offense.

***

My good friend, Tammy Faye, shared a story about the torture of harboring offense. She likened the offense to a punishment that was used to bring judgment upon a murderer many centuries ago.

The dead body was attached to the murderer; chained to them, they were forced to carry the corpse around until the stench and rottenness of the deceased ate its way through the perpetrator resulting in death.

There is an awful torment to offense that the offended one is incapable of seeing.

You must learn to recognize the characteristics of offense to keep from becoming a victim.

Most people do not know when they are truly offended, let alone know the characteristics of offense. Purpose in your heart to learn these characteristics, so you will never fall prey to its treacherous works.

Get the dead man off your back and choose to forgive.

TEN

The Characteristics of Offense

❧

The Characteristics of Offense

Where the Spirit of the Lord is, there is liberty. You do not have to be held in bondage to religion, traditions of men, or the oppression of Satan. Jesus said, "I am come that they might have life, and that they might have it more abundantly." (John 10:10b) God wants you to live a life of abundance.

Abundance in your finances.

Abundance in your marriage.

Abundance in your relationships.

Abundance in all you do.

That is God's plan for your life. The only thing that can keep you from enjoying this kind of life is the bitter root of offense.

How many Christians do you know who are surrounded by blessings and still complain of the misery they live in? They claim that Satan is continually stealing from them, robbing them of their health. Quite the contrary, Satan does not have the power to bring anything upon a child of God except he be given permission.

It is not that people are not praying enough. They may fast and read their Bibles; but when offense is present, it gives permission for jealousy, pride, and a number of other evils to work against all their efforts. In most cases, the destruction viewed as an onslaught from Satan is really self-inflicted.

Satan is no match to our God. He is neither His equal nor His counterpart.

He is Satan.

He is Lucifer cast out from Heaven, a fallen angel, and a defeated foe.

He himself is offended:

Offended at God...

Offended at himself...

Offended at his derelict existence.

Remember, Jesus said, "I beheld Satan cast out of Heaven like a bolt of lightning." Allow me to make an interesting observation. When a bolt of lightning has been activated, it is finished. It is over; it cannot strike again. That same bolt of lightning will never be seen again.

When Jesus went to the cross, He took care of the problem for the last time. At that point, Satan's work was finished. His power was seen briefly, and then, abruptly stripped forever just like the bolt of lightning.

The only way Satan can gain advantage over a believer

is through the eventual self-destruction produced by offense.

I know what you must be thinking right about now. Perhaps, you are contemplating the Scripture over in the book of II Corinthians 2:11 that reads, "Lest Satan should get an advantage of us: for we are not ignorant of his devices." This passage may give you the idea that Satan is very tricky, and that we should be watchful because he could ensnare us.

The Apostle Paul was testing the attitude of the believers to see if they would be obedient and altogether agreeable in everything.

Take some time, read the subsequent passages, and discover the evil that was pervading the minds of this local congregation. (I Corinthians 5:1)

Paul wanted to know if they could forgive the man in their congregation who had committed incest. The people were offended at the immorality of this individual; and in the process, they were rooting themselves deeply into offense.

The characteristics of offense are not always as we suppose. Many times, offense hides behind a false confidence. People walk around hiding behind their jesting; when all the while, they are deeply offended.

Paul urged the believers at Corinth to forgive for the purpose of not giving Satan an opportunity to gain advantage over them. Unforgiveness was the door to Satan's invasion. It was not that he had a super-power working for him; instead, their weakness made them vulnerable and him, assumedly, strong.

Offense can give way to satanic activity.

The doorway to satanic attack is forged through unforgiveness and offense. Bitterness, unforgiveness, and offense loom their destructive forces together to bring, ultimately, death.

This places a greater consequence on offense than, even, the vilest sins.

The man was found having an affair with his stepmother. Notice the Apostle Paul's tone as he admonishes the people to forgive the perpetrator. He says, "But if someone [the one among you who committed incest] has caused [all this] grief and pain, he has caused it not to me, but in some measure, not to put it too severely, [he has distressed] all of you. For such a one this censure by the majority [which he has received is] sufficient [punishment]." (II Corinthians 2:5,6 AMP) The perpetrator had suffered enough by being removed from the fellowship. He goes on to say in verse seven, "So [instead of further rebuke, now] you should rather turn and [graciously] forgive and comfort and encourage [him], to keep him from being overwhelmed by excessive sorrow and despair." Paul pleads with them to forgive this man and to be free from offense.

The battle is not in the flesh or the acts of the flesh, rather, in the heart.

The war of all wars was waged in Heaven. No longer do we have to fight; the battle was won, and the war is over! Christ has already overcome the enemy. He fought for you and for me.

The fight continues in the Heavenlies, in the principalities, in high places; but it is not a war we engage in. The conflict is not taking place in the realm of flesh and blood but in the realm of the Heavenlies.

What then is the position of the believer in warfare? We are called to take on the whole armor of God, so we may be able to resist in the evil day all things and stand firm.

The Greek word for withstand according to Strong's Concordance is *anthistemic* meaning: to stand against, to oppose, to resist. This word comes from the root word *histemi,* which means: to abide, appoint, bring, continue, covenant, establish, and hold up. In other words, stay where you are, stay in covenant agreement, and resist the devil. Do not engage in his fight.

James 4:7 says, "Submit yourselves therefore to God. **Resist** the devil, and he will flee from you." Resist means: to defy; the implication given here is to, simply, ignore Satan and his ploys. There is no warfare involved with this kind of stance against the devil; it simply means resist.

Can you imagine the devil's response if believers would simply stand in agreement with the Scriptures, with each other, with their purpose, and with their destiny and stare blankly at his wild antics? He would not know what to do. It would totally ruin his strategy of barking, ranting, and raving. The Bible says, he [the devil] is as a roaring lion, seeking whom he may devour.

It is a known fact; when confronted with the assault of any type of beast, the last thing to do is run. The best strategy is to remain motionless.

Yet, Christians rant and rave back at this roaring lion and end up being mauled.

You may be thinking about the Scripture that speaks of Satan throwing his darts at the believers. These darts cannot penetrate the armor of God. The only way they can get past the armor is from behind.

A study in armors of that era proves that the armor simply covered the front part of the body. The backside was completely exposed. Consequently, if you were caught running from your enemy, you were vulnerable to his assaults against you.

The armor of God, as described in the book of Ephesians, covers you from your head down to your feet. Not one dart that Satan directs at you can prosper as long as you are marching in a forward motion.

If you are always on the defensive waiting for your

enemy to attack, you will find yourself running every time. You cannot wait for Satan to attack you. The best offensive strategy against the devil is through your worship.

Scripture states that for this purpose was the Son of God manifest to destroy the works of the devil.

Too many precious believers spend much of their time running from the devil.

When you are positioned for victory through the knowledge of the Word, the power of the Holy Ghost, and the weapon of worship; you are assured victory every time!

Victory is not simply an outward manifestation of success, rather, an inward state that carries you through to completion.

On the outside, some people look churchy and holy. They may raise their hands in worship, and everything may look right, while on the inside, they are filled with envy and strife. Victory is nowhere in sight. The Book of James says, "Where envy and strife is, every evil work abounds." Their bills may be paid, they may be driving a new car, and in good health, but victorious living still eludes them because of envy and strife.

Therefore, the real war is taking place in the hearts and minds of God's people. God looks at the heart of man, not at the stupid mistakes one makes in the flesh.

We are always going to make mistakes.

We are always going to war against this flesh.

We are never going to be righteous enough, holy enough, or clean enough in our flesh to come before God. Each time we stand before Him, our righteousness is as filthy rags.

The characteristics of offense are not always visible on a person's countenance. A smile, raised hands, or even laughter can be the masquerade for the dark secret burning in the hearts of many. On the outside, there is joy and happiness;

while on the inside, they are filled with malice, hatred, jealousies, divisions, and pride.

How does one identify this secret sin?

How can you know you are not buried deep in offense?

Have you ever been so enamored with a pastor only to find yourself out of sorts with him the first time he steps on your toes with his preaching? If you do not yield your spirit to the Holy Spirit, you can easily become offended. Before you know it, this same man who at one time represented all that is good, now, represents evil.

People may pray in tongues and speak evil of their pastors based on what he preached on Sunday morning move into offense. Their defense becomes their good works. They serve on the board, they teach Sunday School, they tithe, and give money; but what does it profit them? Their worship goes unheard and unnoticed by God.

They now seek to invalidate what was once Godly and beneficial to them. They view the same man with an attitude of contempt.

This is a perfect example of double-mindedness. You try to invalidate what was once valuable to you. You change your mind based on your offense. You are not suspicious by nature, but you are offended, and you begin to question the motives of your man of God.

People who have to question everything...

"But why do we have to do this or that?"

"Why do I have to submit?" These kinds of people who always have a question about instruction are usually the ones who will rise up against their leaders. Offense does not want anybody telling it what to do.

Many believers are living in denial, not wanting to accept the fact that many of their problems are because of their choices and not the fault of Satan. Without the proper teaching and instruction, people continue to paddle their way through their rivers of offense much like the deceptive appearance of the Amazon, which appears tranquil as it flows steadily down stream. Underneath there is an assemblage of deadly, poisonous animal life: piranhas, snakes, crocodiles and, even, the largest of all snakes - the dreaded anaconda.

Offense is like the attack of an anaconda. It attacks its victim with an unexpected bite, wraps itself around its prey, and stealthily begins to squeeze the life out of it.

A few years ago, there was a woman who went through all the big name ministries. She graced the stages of all the great men of faith that we know. She had some kind of ministry where she would leave a spot of oil where she stood. She had blood come out of her back, and she would drop feathers, which were supposedly the representation of the Holy Spirit. She was later exposed. The startling revelation was soon made that she had been using pigeon feathers, and her ministry was a big hoax.

All kinds of miracles were taking place in the midst of these boldfaced lies. No one was the smarter, when it came to questioning, whether or not this ministry lined up with the Scriptures.

The works of Satan will be displayed in the form of counterfeit miracles amidst our worship to God. Deception cannot be discerned in the midst of deception.

Evil is not evil until there is good to provide a contrast. The deceptive works of darkness can only be distinguished against the backdrop of holiness and light.

Bad things happening to Christians are not always the works of darkness. There are times when God is proving and testing His people. You are not always going to get out of your circumstances immediately. There are times when you must persevere, endure, and rejoice in your suffering even as Christ suffered for us.

I am a man of faith. I walk in divine health, but there are times when there is a testing that comes upon me. I could rebuke, fast, and have the intercessors pray against the works of darkness; but many times, God is in the testing!

"You were running a good race. Who cut in on you and kept you from obeying the truth?"

Who is behind this? The Apostle Paul probes.

"That kind of persuasion does not come from the one who calls you. A little yeast works through the whole batch of dough."

One offended individual can inflict pain on an entire congregation, causing the church to split or completely disseminate.

"You were doing well. You were serving well.

What happened? Who cut in on you?" He continues. It does not say, "Oh, the devil deceived you."

I am confident in the Lord that you will take no other view.

The one who is throwing you into confusion will pay the penalty, whoever he may be.

If Paul knew it was a satanic attack, he would have said so.

He then says, "Brothers, if I am still preaching circumcision, why am I still being persecuted?

In that case, the offense of the cross has been abolished.

As for those agitators, I wish they would go the whole way and emasculate themselves!" In other words, he wished they would be removed completely from among the others.

Paul was not playing around with these words. "You, my brothers, were called to be free. But do not use your freedom to indulge in the sinful nature; rather, serve one another in love." (Galatians 5:7-9,11-13 NIV)

Wisdom Principle: Obedience Without Agreement Is Oppression.

Servitude is not simply an outlet for those who are called to serve; it is as much a part of the character of Christ as love is. We are all called to serve one another.

If you have difficulty serving others, you will have difficulty worshiping the Lord. Jesus' response to Satan when He was tempted in the desert was from the Old Testament Scripture: "Thou shalt worship the Lord thy God, and him only shalt thou serve." Serving follows worship.

Serving others is the nature of a true worshiper. We cannot truly say we love the Lord and hate one another.

Be careful what kind of attitude you take when serving others; it could be caustic to your worship.

As you read along in The Secret you will soon be convinced of the assignment of offense. It is the only thing that can keep you from truly worshiping the Lord.

It is like a cancer that eats away at the virtue the Holy Spirit produces in you for the purpose of offering pure worship to the Lord.

How sad that many people sitting in churches with offense in their hearts desire to honour the Lord. They may lift their hands in worship to the Lord, but it is not acceptable worship. They offer up strange fire in the guise of true worship.

ELEVEN

Strange Fire

DR. THOMAS MICHAEL

The Secret

FOREWORD BY DR. JIM AMMERMAN